OTHER BOOKS BY JUNE JORDAN:

Who Look at Me
Soulscript
The Voice of the Children
Some Changes
His Own Where
Dry Victories
Fannie Lou Hamer
New Days: Poems of Exile and Return
New Life: New Room

THINGS THAT I DO
IN THE DARK

THINGS THAT I

Random House New York

DO IN THE DARK

Selected Poetry by *June Jordan*

Library of Congress Cataloging in Publication Data
Jordan, June, 1936-
Things that I do in the dark.
I. Title.
PS3560.073A6   1977   811'.5'4   76-53498
ISBN 0-394-40937-X
ISBN 0-394-73327-4 pbk.

Selections in this book have been previously published in
New Days by June Jordan, *Some Changes* by June Jordan,
*Transatlantic Review, Iowa Review, Hoodoo #4, Mother
Jones, Ms. Magazine, Black World, National Lawyer's
Guild Newsletter, Mother & Child*, ed. by Mary Lawrence
(Thomas Y. Crowell Company, Inc. 1975).

Grateful acknowledgment is made to Thomas Y. Crowell
Company, Inc. for permission to reprint "Who Look At Me"
from *Who Look At Me* by June Jordan. Copyright © 1969
by June Jordan. Reprinted by permission.

Manufactured in the United States of America

9 8 7 6 5 4 3 2

FIRST EDITION

Dedicated
to the liberation of all my love
and
to the memory of Granville I. Jordan
who fathered many dreams
and
to the memory of Mildred M. Jordan
whose sacrifice I hope to vindicate
and
to life itself

These poems
they are things that I do
in the dark
reaching for you
whoever you are
and
are you ready?

These words
they are stones in the water
running away

These skeletal lines
they are desperate arms for my longing and love.

I am a stranger
learning to worship the strangers
around me

whoever you are
whoever I may become.

*With gratitude for the beautiful work of the writer
Toni Morrison, who, as my editor, has kept on believing
this book into print.*

And with loving to Patricia, who helps me keep the faith.

j.j.

CONTENTS

DIRECTED BY DESIRE

AGAINST THE STILLWATERS

TOWARDS A PERSONAL SEMANTICS

FOR MY OWN

WHO LOOK AT ME
Dedicated to my son, Christopher

Who would paint a people
black or white?

*

For my own I have held
where nothing showed me how
where finally I left alone
to trace another destination

*

A white stare splits the air
by blindness on the subway
in department stores
The Elevator
          (that unswerving ride
where man ignores the brother
by his side)

A white stare splits obliterates
the nerve-wrung wrist from work
the breaking ankle or
the turning glory
of a spine

*

Is that how we look to you
a partial nothing clearly real?

Who see a solid clarity
of feature
size and shape of some
one head
an unmistaken nose

the fact of afternoon
as darkening
his candle eyes

Older men with swollen neck

2: Things That I Do in the Dark

(when they finally sit down
who will stand up
for them?)

I cannot remember nor imagine pretty
people treat me
like a doublejointed stick
                    WHO LOOK AT ME
                    WHO SEE

the tempering sweetness
of a little girl who wears
her first pair of earrings
and a red dress

the grace of a boy removing
a white mask he makes beautiful

Iron grille across the glass
and frames of motion closed or
charred or closed

The axe lies on the ground
She listening to his coming sound

Him
just touching his feet
powerful and wary

anonymous and normal
parents and their offspring
posed in formal
                    *
I am
impossible to explain
remote from old and new interpretations
and yet
not exactly
                    *
look at the stranger as

he lies more gray than black
on that colorquilt
that

3: For My Own

(everyone will say)
seems bright beside him

look
black sailors on the light
green sea the sky keeps blue
the wind blows high
and hard at night
for anyhow anywhere new

              *

Who see starvation at the table
lines of men no work to do
my mother ironing a shirt?

Who see a frozen skin the midnight
of the winter and the hallway cold
to kill you like the dirt?

where kids buy soda pop
in shoeshine parlors
barber shops so they can hear
some laughing

Who look at me?

Who see the children
on their street the torn down door the wall
complete an early losing
                           games of ball
the search to find
a fatherhood a mothering of mind
a multimillion multicolored mirror
of an honest humankind?

              *

look close
and see me black man mouth
for breathing (North and South)
A MAN

I am black alive and looking back at you.

              *

4: Things That I Do in the Dark

see me brown girl throat
that throbs from servitude

see me hearing fragile
leap
and lead a black boy
reckless to succeed
to wrap my pride
around tomorrow and to go
there
without fearing

see me darkly covered ribs
around my heart across my skull
thin skin protects the part
that dulls from longing
*
Who see the block we face
the thousand miles of solid alabaster space
inscribed keep off keep out don't touch
and Wait Some More for Half as Much?
*
To begin is no more agony
than opening your hand
*
sometimes you have to dance
like spelling
the word joyless
*
Describe me broken mast
adrift but strong
regardless what may
come along
*
What do you suppose he hears
every evening?
*
I am stranded in a hungerland
of great prosperity
*

5: For My Own

shelter happens seldomly and
like an accident
it stops

*

No doubt
the jail is white where I was born
but black will bail me out

*

We have lived as careful
as a church and prayer
in public

*

we reveal
a complicated past
of tinderbox and ruin
where we carried water
for the crops

we come from otherwhere

victim to a rabid cruel cargo crime

to separate and rip apart
the trusting members of one heart

my family

I looked for you
I looked for you

*

(slavery:) the insolence

came to frontiers
of paralyze highways
freedom strictly underground

came here to hatred hope labor love
and lynchlength rope

came a family to a family

I found my father
silently despite the grieving
fury of his life

6: Things That I Do in the Dark

Afternoons he wore his hat
and held a walking stick

I found my mother
her geography
becomes our home

                *

so little safety
almost nowhere like the place
that childhood plans
in a pounding happy space
between deliberate brown and clapping
hands
that preached a reaping to the wildly
    sleeping earth
brown hands that worked for rain a fire inside
    and food to eat
from birth brown hands
    to hold

                *

New energies of darkness we
disturbed a continent
like seeds

and life grows slowly
so we grew

We became a burly womb
an evening harvest kept by prayers
a hallelujah little room

We grew despite the crazy killing scorn
that broke the brightness to be born

In part we grew
by looking back at you

that white terrain
impossible for black America to thrive
that hostile soil to mazelike toil
backbreaking people into pain

7: *For My Own*

we grew by work by waiting
to be seen
black face black body and black mind
beyond obliterating
homicide of daily insult daily death
the pistol slur the throbbing redneck war
with breath

In part we grew
with heroes who could halt a slaveship
lead the crew
like Cinque (son
of a Mendi African Chief) he
led in 1839
the Amistad Revolt
from slavehood forced
a victory he
killed the captain killed the cook
took charge
a mutiny for manhood
people
called him killer but
some
the Abolitionists
looked back at robbery
of person
murdering of spirit
slavery requires
and one
John Quincy Adams (seventy-three)
defended Cinque who
by highest court decree
in 1841 stood free
and freely he returned
to Africa
victorious

In part we grew
grandmother husband son
together when the laborblinding day was done

8: *Things That I Do in the Dark*

In part we grew
as we were meant to grow
ourselves
with kings and queens no white man knew

we grew by sitting on a stolen chair
by windows and a dream
by setting up a separate sail
to carry life
to start the song

to stop the scream
                    *
These times begin the ending of all lies
the fantasies of seasons start and stop
the circle leads to no surprise
for death does not bewilder
only life can kill can mystify can start
and stop like flowers ripening a funeral
like (people) holding hands across the knife
that cuts the casket to an extraordinary size
                    *
Tell the whiplash helmets GO!
and take away
that cream and orange Chevrolet
stripped to inside steel and parked
forever on one wheel

Set the wild dogs chewing up
that pitiful capitulation
plastic flower plastic draperies
to dust the dirt

Break the clothesline
Topple down the clotheslinepole

O My Lives Among The Wounded Buildings
should be dressed in trees and grass
                    *
we will no longer wait for want for watch
for what we will

9: For My Own

*

we make a music marries room to room.

*

listen to that new girl
tears her party dress to sweep
the sidewalk as the elderly slow
preacher nears the mailbox in a black suit
emptyhanded

*

Although the world
forgets me
I will say yes
AND NO

*

NO
to a carnival run by freaks
who take a life
and tie it terrible
behind my back

*

No One Exists As Number Two
If you deny it you should try
being someone number two

*

I want to hear something other than a single
ringing on the concrete

*

I grieve the sorrow roar the sorrow sob
of many more left hand or right
black children and white
men the mountaintop the mob
I grieve the sorrow roar the sorrow sob
the fractured staring at the night

Sometimes America the shamescape
knock-rock territory losing shape
the Southern earth like blood
rolls valleys cold gigantic
weeping willow flood

10: Things That I Do in the Dark

that lunatic that lovely land
that graveyard growing
trees remark where men
another black man
died he died again
he died

          *

I trust you will remember how we tried to love
above the pocket deadly need to please
and how so many of us died there
on our knees

          *

Who see the roof and corners of my pride
to be (as you are) free?

WHO LOOK AT ME?

                                      1968

FOR CHRISTOPHER

Tonight
    the machinery of shadow
        moves into the light

He is lying there
      not a true invalid
            not dying

Now his face looks blue
        but all of that small body
           will more than do
                as life.

The lady radiologist
          regardless how and where
              she turns the knob

will never know
            the plenty of pain
                        growing

parts to arm
        a man inside the boy

practically asleep

1967

JULY 4, 1974
(Washington, D.C.)

At least it helps me to think about my son
a Leo/born to us
(Aries and Cancer) some
sixteen years ago
in St. Johns Hospital next to the Long Island
Railroad tracks
Atlantic Avenue/Brooklyn
New York

at dawn

which facts
do not really prepare you
(do they)

for him

angry
serious
and running through the darkness with his own

becoming light

1974

ALL THE WORLD MOVED

All the world moved next to me strange
I grew on my knees
in hats and taffeta trusting
the holy water to run
like grief from a brownstone
cradling.

Blessing a fear of the anywhere
face too pale to be family
my eyes wore ribbons
for Christ on the subway
as weekly as holiness
in Harlem.

God knew no East no West no South
no Skin nothing I learned like
traditions of sin but later
life began and strangely
I survived His innocence
without my own.

1964

FROM AN UPROOTED CONDITION

In the house of my son I am hiding myself
who will not tell anybody
that love lies behind or before
this need when no one
is near to her

sometimes the poem tends to repeat itself
the subject is screaming and sad
and the hours do not belong or allow

Pitiless
she watches the stranger
she thinks that at least he
comes from someplace
that gave him permission to leave

She is taking small steps
and making small noises that melt in the air
easily
easily
there is nowhere that she can go
and her hands are frozen hard
in this
absolutely new
position
                    more or less
we know the attitude the forms
of childbirth and of dying

what
is the right way the womanly expression
of the infinitive that fights
infinity

to abort?

1971

UNCLE BULLBOY

His brother   after dinner
once a year would play the piano
short and tough in white shirt
plaid suspenders   green tie and
checked trousers.
Two teeth were gold. His eyes
were pink with alcohol. His fingers
thumped for Auld Lang Syne.

14: Things That I Do in the Dark

He played St. Louis Woman
Boogie, Blues, the light
pedestrian.

      But one night after dinner
after chitterlings and pigs' feet
after bourbon rum and rye
after turnip greens and mustard greens
and sweet potato pie
Bullboy looking everywhere
realized his brother was not there.

Who would emphasize the luxury
of ice cream by the gallon who would
repeat effusively the glamour not the gall
of five degrees outstanding on the wall?
Which head would nod and then recall
the crimes   the apples stolen from the stalls
the soft coal stolen by the pile?
Who would admire
the eighteenth pair of forty
dollar shoes?
Who could extol their mother with good
brandy as his muse?

      His brother   dead from drinking
Bullboy drank to clear his thinking
saw the roach inside the riddle.
Soon the bubbles from his glass
were the only bits of charm
which overcame his folded arms.

                                    1965

FOR MY JAMAICAN SISTER A LITTLE BIT LOST ON THE ISLAND OF MANHATTAN

small
and glowing in this cold place
of brick
   cement
   dry sand
   and
   broken glass
where there are waters
of the earth
flowing like love alive
you will make them warm
waters
hot (even)
like the delicate sweat
of tiger lilies
blowing about
barely in flame
           at sunrise

1975

ON HOLIDAYS IN THE BEST TRADITION

Thanksgiving is a good time to stuff
a T.W.A. Ambassador turkey flight
to Las Vegas
now leaving
       the family
       the friends

at 500 miles per hour
the pilot explains that

16: Things That I Do in the Dark

"knowledge of this procedure
will definitely expedite survival"

(so that's cool)

now leaving
            the family
            the friends

to fasten your eyes
on the positively most
enormous
high billboard signal calls
for HELP

now leaving
(for)
      money money
      money money money

neon names and neon numbers
neon blink blank

here is a store on the street in Las Vegas
"Selling Indian Jewelry Since 1957"
but
here are no Indians in Las Vegas
since you know
the other people have arrived
the hearts spades clubs and diamonds
mixed up
alone and gambling
everybody stretched out on the dark
felt wheel
fuzzy cowboys teachers Black folks white folks
almost
all the American stuffing
of the all American turkey
tricked out lonely
gambling
ringading ding
ringading dingdong

17: For My Own

dingaling
money
money

now leaving
        the family
        the friends

                                1972

JUICE OF A LEMON ON THE TRAIL OF LITTLE YELLOW

Little Yellow looked at the banana tree and
he looked at the moon and he heard a banana tree baboon
beneath the moon and he sat on the grass
and fell asleep there

Little Yellow nine years old underneath the moon beside
a big banana tree smiled a mango smile as he
listened to a lullabye palm and a naked woman broke
coconuts for him and fed him meat from her mango
mammaries

Little Yellow curled himself in a large banana leaf
and he deeply sailed asleep toward the mango moon
Little Yellow traveled to a place where coolies worked
to build a bathtub for the rough and tribal Caribbean

There on that lush cerulean plateau and trapped he
was kept by his boss brother who positively took
out his teeth and left the mango mouth of Little Yellow
empty

                                1963

CLOCK ON HANCOCK STREET

In the wintertime my father wears a hat
a green straw laundry shrunken hat
to open up the wartime iron gate
requiring a special key he keeps
in case he hears the seldom basement bell
a long key cost him seven dollars
took three days to make

around the corner

in the house no furniture remains
he gave away the piano
and the hard-back parlor couch the rosy rug
and the double bed
the large black bureau
china cups and saucers
from Japan

His suitcase is a wooden floor
where magazines called *Life*
smell like a garbage truck
that travels farther than he
reasonably can expect
to go

His face seems small or
loose and bearded in the afternoon

Today he was complaining about criminals:

They will come and steal the heavy red umbrella stand

from upstairs in the hallway
where my mother used to walk

and talk to him

1969

19: For My Own

POEM FOR GRANVILLE IVANHOE JORDAN
November 4, 1890–December 21, 1974
Dedicated to Stephen Henderson

I

At the top of your tie
the dressy maroon number
with one/small
gravy stain
remaining

the knot is now too narrow for your neck

a ridiculous a dustfree/shiny box confines
your arms and legs
accustomed to a boxer's hunch a wrestler's hauling
energies at partial rest

3 or 4 A.M. a thousand nights
who stubbornly retrieved your own
into
illumination
> bright beyond blindfiling of
> a million letters at the Post Office which
> never forwarded even one
> of a hundred
> fantasies
> your kitchenkept plans
keeping you awake

West Indian in kitchen exile
alone between the days
and studying the National Geographic Magazines
white explorations and
excitement
in the places you were forced to leave

> no shoes
> no teeth

but oxlike shoulders
and hazel eyes that watered
slightly
from the reading you did teach yourself to do

West Indian in kitchen exile
omnivorous consumer of thick
kitchen table catalogs
of seeds for sale
for red
bright flowers

seeds

slick and colorful
on the quick
lush pages
advertising pear and
apple trees
or peaches
in first bloom

        who saved for money orders
        for the flowers
        for the trees
        who used a spade
        and shovel
        heavily and well
        to plant the Brooklyn backyard
        innocent of all
        the succulent
        the gorgeous schemes
        you held between your fingers
        like a simple
        piece of paper

Jesus, Daddy
what did you expect

an orange grove
a eucalyptus
roses

from the cities that despised the sweet calypso
of your trust?

II

Who stole the mustache from your face?
It's gone.
Who took it away?
Why did you stop there

>   *on your knees*

at eighty four

>   *a man*

down on your knees

>   *in inconceivable but willing*
>   *prayer/your life*
>   *God's baby in gray hair*

What pushed you from your own two feet?

>   *my father*

III

To this you have come

>   *a calm a concrete pit*
contains your corpse
above the spumespent ending of the surf
against the mountain trees and fertile pitch
of steeply clinging dirt

>   *"Sleep on Beloved*
>   *Take Thy Rest"*

the minister
eyes bare beneath the island light
intones a feeling mumbo jumbo

22: Things That I Do in the Dark

"ashes to ashes
dust to dust"

the village men
wrists strained to lumped up veins and cartilage
(from carrying the casket)
do not pray
they do not sing

"A-bide with me,
fast falls the eventide"

It's afternoon
It's hot
It's lit by sun that cannot be undone

by death

1974

AFTER READING THE NUMBER ONE
INTELLECTUAL AMERICAN BEST SELLER,
FUTURE SHOCK, ALL ABOUT CHANGE
IS WHERE WE'RE AT

Well
Number Two
Baby
Is That Change Ain' Nowhere
You Can Hold On

Now Read That
Now Read This

gone
gone
Eddie
gone
Greg

23: For My Own

gone
Julius
Millen
Peter
Alice
Frances
Terri
gone
Aunt
Uncle
Cousins
Niece and Nephew
Father
Mother
Son
GONE
GONE
Dale
Primus
Clarence
Ross
GONE
GONE
Damn. Don'
give me no garbage
about
DIS IS DUH FUTURE
speed up
travel
turn around
make it mobile
hit the road

shit
I'm just tired saying good-bye

1972

ONE MINUS ONE MINUS ONE
(This is a first map of territory
I will have to explore as poems,
again and again)

My mother murdering me
to have a life of her own

What would I say
(if I could speak about it?)

My father raising me
to be a life that he
owns

What can I say
(in this loneliness)

1976

FOR MY MOTHER

for my mother
I would write a list
of promises so solid
loafing fish and onions
okra palm tree coconut
and Khus-Khus paradise
would
hard among the mongoose
enemies delight
a neo-noon-night trick
prosperity

for my father
I would decorate a doorway
weaving women into the daytime
of his travel also

25: For My Own

season the snow to rice and peas
to peppery pearls on a flowering
platter drunkards stilt
at breakfast bacchanalia
swaying swift or stubborn
coral rocks
regenerate

for my only love
I would stop the silence

one of these days

won't come too soon
when the blank
familias blank
will fold away
a highly inflammable
balloon eclipsed by seminal
and nubile

loving

1969

ON THE SPIRT OF MILDRED JORDAN

After sickness and a begging
from her bed
my mother dressed herself
grey lace-up oxfords
stockings baggy on her shrunken legs
an orange topper
rhinestone buttons
and a powder blue straw
hat with plastic
flowers

Then
she took the street
in short steps toward the corner

chewing gum
no less

she let the family laugh
again

she wasn't foxy
she was strong

1971

GETTIN DOWN TO GET OVER
Dedicated to my mother

MOMMA MOMMA MOMMA
momma momma
mammy
nanny
granny
woman
mistress
sista

luv

blackgirl
slavegirl

gal

honeychile
sweetstuff
sugar
sweetheart
baby
Baby Baby

27: For My Own

MOMMA MOMMA
Black Momma
Black bitch
Black pussy
piecea tail
nice piecea ass

hey daddy! hey
bro!
we walk together (an')
talk together (an')
dance and *do*
(together)
dance and do/hey!
daddy!
bro!
hey!
nina nikki nonni nommo nommo
momma Black
Momma

Black Woman
Black
Female Head of Household
Black Matriarchal Matriarchy
Black Statistical
Lowlife Lowlevel Lowdown
Lowdown and *up*
to be Low-down
Black Statistical
Low Factor
Factotem
Factitious Fictitious
Figment Figuring in Lowdown Lyin
Annual Reports

Black Woman/Black
Hallelujah Saintly
patient
smilin

humble
givin thanks
for
Annual Reports and
Monthly Dole
and
Friday night
and
(*good* God!)
Monday mornin: Black and Female
martyr masochist
(A BIG WHITE LIE)
Momma Momma

What does Mothafuckin mean?
WHO'S THE MOTHAFUCKA
FUCKED MY MOMMA
messed yours over
and right now
be trippin on my starveblack
female soul
a macktruck
mothafuck
the first primordial
the paradig/digmatic
dogmatistic mothafucka who
is he?
hey!
momma momma

dry eyes on the
shy/dark/hidden/cryin Black
face
of the loneliness
the rape
the brokeup mailbox
an' no western union roses
come inside the kitchen
and no poem
take you through the whole night

29: For My Own

and no big
Black
burly
hand
be holdin yours
to have to hold onto
no
big Black burly hand
no nommo
no Black prince
come riding from the darkness
on a beautiful black horse
no bro
no daddy

"I was sixteen when I met my father.
In a bar.
In Baltimore.
He told me who he was
and what he does.
Paid for the drinks.
I looked.
I listened.
And I left him.
It was civil
perfectly
and absolute bull
shit.
The drinks was leakin waterweak
and never got down to my knees."

hey daddy
what they been and done to you
and what you been and done
to me
to momma
momma momma
hey
sugar daddy
big daddy

sweet daddy
Black Daddy
The Original Father Divine
the everlovin
deep
tall
bad
buck
jive
cold
strut
bop
split
tight
loose
close
hot
hot
hot
sweet SWEET DADDY
WHERE YOU BEEN AND
WHEN YOU COMIN BACK TO ME
HEY
WHEN YOU COMIN BACK
TO MOMMA
momma momma

And Suppose He Finally Say
"Look, Baby.
I Loves Me Some
Everything about You.
Let Me Be Your Man."
That reach around the hurtin
like a dream.
And I ain never wakin up
from that one.
momma momma
momma momma

II

Consider the Queen

hand on her hip
sweat restin from
the corn/bean/greens' field
steamy under the pale/sly
suffocatin sun

Consider the Queen

she fix the cufflinks
on his Sunday shirt
and fry some chicken
bake some cake
and tell the family
"Never mine about the bossman
don' know how a human
bein spozed to act. Jus'
never mind about him.
Wash your face.
Sit down. And let
the good Lord bless this table."

Consider the Queen

her babies pullin at the nipples
pullin at the momma milk

the infant fingers gingerly
approach caress the
soft/Black/swollen/momma breast

and there
inside the mommasoft
life-spillin treasure chest
the heart
breaks

rage by grief by sorrow
weary weary
breaks

breaks quiet
silently
the weary sorrow
quiet now the furious
the adamant the broken
busted beaten down and beaten up
the beaten beaten beaten
weary heart beats
tender-steady
and the babies suck/
the seed of blood
and love glows at the
soft/Black/swollen momma breast

Consider the Queen

she works when she works
in the laundry *in jail*
in the school house *in jail*
in the office *in jail*
on the soap box *in jail*
on the desk
on the floor
on the street
on the line
at the door
lookin fine
at the head of the line
steppin sharp from behind
in the light
with a song
wearing boots
or a belt
and a gun
drinkin wine when it's time

when the long week is done
but she works when she works
in the laundry in jail
she works when she works

33: For My Own

Consider the Queen

she sleeps when she sleeps
with the king in the kingdom
she
sleeps when she sleeps
with the wall
with whatever it is who happens
to call
with me and with you
(to survive you make
do/you explore more and more)
so she sleeps when she sleeps
a really deep sleep

Consider the Queen

a full/Black/glorious/a purple rose
aroused by the tiger breathin
beside her
a shell with the moanin
of ages inside her
a hungry one feedin the folk
what they need

Consider the Queen.

III

Blackman
let that white girl go
She know what you ought to know.
(By now.)

IV

MOMMA MOMMA
momma momma
family face
face of the family alive

momma
mammy
momma
woman
sista
baby
luv

the house on fire/
poison waters/
earthquake/
and the air a nightmare/
turn
turn
turn around the
national gross product
growin
really gross/turn
turn
turn the pestilence away
the miserable killers
and Canarsie
Alabama
people beggin to be people
warfare on the welfare
of the folk/
hey
turn
turn away
the trickbag university/the
trickbag propaganda/
trickbag
tricklins of prosperity/of
pseudo-"status"
lynchtree necklace
on the strong
round
neck of you
my momma

35: For My Own

momma momma
turn away
the f.b.i./the state police/the cops/
the/everyone of the
infest/incestuous investigators
into you
and Daddy/into us
hey
turn
my mother
turn
the face of history
to your own
and please be smilin
if you can
be smilin
at the family

momma momma

let the funky forecast
be the last
one we will ever
want to listen to

And Daddy see
the stars fall down
and burn a light
into the singin
darkness of your eyes
my Daddy
my Blackman
you take my body in
your arms/you use
the oil of coconuts/of trees and
flowers/fish and new fruits
from the new world
to enflame me in this otherwise
cold place
please

36: *Things That I Do in the Dark*

meanwhile
momma
momma momma
teach me how to kiss
the king within the kingdom
teach me how to t.c.b./to make do
and be
like you
teach me to survive my
momma
teach me how to hold a new life
momma
help me
turn the face of history
to your face.

1972

AH, MOMMA

Ah, Momma,

Did the house ever know the night-time of your spirit: the flash and flame of you who once, when we crouched in what you called "the little room," where your dresses hung in their pallid colorings—an uninteresting row of uniforms—and where there were dusty, sweet-smelling boxes of costume jewelry that nevertheless shone like rubies, gold, and diamonds, once, in that place where the secondhand mirror blurred the person, dull, that place without windows, with doors instead of walls, so that your small-space most resembled a large and rather hazardous closet, once, in there you told me, whispering, that once, you had wanted to be an artist: someone, you explained, who could just boldly go and sit near the top of a hill and watch the setting of the sun
Ah, Momma!
You said this had been your wish when you were quite as

young as I was then: a twelve- or thirteen-year-old girl who heard your confidence with terrified amazement: what had happened to you and your wish? Would it happen to me too?

Ah, Momma:
"The little room" of your secrets, your costumery, perfumes and photographs of an old boyfriend you did not marry (for reasons not truly clear to me as I saw you make sure, time after time, that his pictures were being kept as clean and as safe as possible)—"the little room" adjoined the kitchen, the kitchen where no mystery survived, except for the mystery of you: woman who covered her thick and long, black hair with a starched, white nurse's cap when she went "on duty" away from our home into the hospital I came to hate, jealously, woman who rolled up her wild and heavy, beautiful hair before she went to bed, woman who tied a headrag around the waving, kinky, well-washed braids, or lengthy, fat curls of her hair while she moved, without particular grace or light, between the table and the stove, between the sink and the table, around and around and around in the spacious, ugly kitchen where she, where you, never dreamed about what you were doing or what you might do instead, and where you taught me to set down plates and silverware, and even fresh-cut flowers from the garden, without appetite, without excitement, without expectation.

It was not there, in that obvious, open, square cookery where you spent most of the hours of the days, it was not there, in the kitchen where nothing ever tasted sweet or sharp enough to sate the yearnings I began to suspect inside your eyes, and also inside the eyes of my father, it was not there that I began to hunger for the sun as my own, legitimate preoccupation; it was not there, in the kitchen, that I began, really, to love you

Ah, Momma,
It was where I found you, hidden away, in your "little room," where your life and the power, the rhythms of your sacrifice, the ritual of your bowed head, and your laughter always partly concealed, where all of you, womanly, reverberated big as the whole house, it was there that I came, humbly, into

an angry, an absolute determination that I would, one day,
prove myself to be, in fact, your daughter
Ah, Momma, I am still trying.

1975

FROM *THE TALKING BACK*
OF MISS VALENTINE JONES:
POEM # ONE

well I wanted to braid my hair
bathe and bedeck my
self so fine
so fully aforethought for
your pleasure
see:
I wanted to travel and read
and runaround fantastic
into war and peace:
I wanted to
surf
dive
fly
climb
conquer
and be conquered
THEN
I wanted to pickup the phone
and find you asking me
if I might possibly be alone
some night
(so I could answer cool
as the jewels I would wear
on bareskin for your
digmedaddy delectation:)
"WHEN
you comin ova?"

39: For My Own

But
I had to remember to write down
margarine on the list
and shoepolish and a can of
sliced pineapples in casea company
and a quarta skim milk cause Teresa's
gainin weight and don' nobody groove on
that much
girl
and next I hadta sort for darks and lights before
the laundry hit the water which I had
to kinda keep a eye on be-
cause if the big hose jumps the sink again that
Mrs. Thompson gointa come upstairs
and brain me with a mop don' smell too
nice even though she hang
it headfirst out the winda
and I had to check
on William like to
burn hisself to death with fever
boy so thin be
callin all day "Momma! Sing to me?"
"Ma! Am I gone die?" and me not
wake enough to sit beside him longer than
to wipeaway the sweat or change the sheets/
his shirt and feed him orange
juice before I fall out sleep and
Sweet My Jesus ain but one can
left
and we not thru the afternoon
and now
you (temporarily) shownup with a thing
you say's a poem and you
call it
"Will The Real Miss Black America Standup?"

                           guilty po' mouth
                           about duty beauties of my
                           headrag

                    boozedup doozies about
                    never mind
                    cause love is blind

well
I can't use it

and the very next bodacious Blackman
call me queen
because my life ain shit
because (in any case) he ain been here to share it
with me
(dish for dish and do for do and
dream for dream)
I'm gone scream him out my house
be-
cause what I wanted was
to braid my hair/bathe and bedeck my
self so fully be-
cause what I wanted was
your love
not pity
be-
cause what I wanted was
your love
your love

                                                    1976

41: For My Own

DIRECTED BY DESIRE

THE ROUND OF GRIEF

Like lonely fools our limbs do not combine.

In some long ago third solstice
    we met: shadows in heat
opening yearn the twinship mouth
    tasting with clean thorn tongue.

Your hand is bone and mine is skin.

Accidents blundered through our space
    falling swallowed behind our face:
the joyful eclipse of alien
    circles measured in assault.

Like lonely fools our limbs do not combine.

Pale with hiding from the burning higher
    than the tree we suckled fearful in the shade:
too late the twilight cooled our eyes
    already blind (believing blindness safe).

Your hand is bone and mine is skin.
Like lonely fools our limbs do not combine.

1954

I LIVE IN SUBTRACTION

I live in subtraction.
I hide from rain.
I hold the sun with sleep.
I sleep without the stars.
I can even close my eyes.

I live in subtraction.
I forget your name.
I forbid my heart its mind.
I forgive my mind its dream.
I can end a dream with death.

1967

POEM IN CELEBRATION OF THE RECOVERY OF MRS. R. BUCKMINSTER FULLER, JUNE, 1967

only nothing limits the world
an intimate an interstitial
following together
from the darkness now
disarms the night
with love
and moves along to open
flights of holding
that will not be blown

1967

IN LOVE

in love

never tired of the forward to retreat
never stayed at the edges
imagining now the full

crack-wrung oblivion rolls
and roars a shifting
certainty

thorns to snare the stars
sea forest firm jaggedly cluster
hard-leaved
bird and bee brambling green
prickle hills of the earth rise
a ready thrust a foamchoke hushing
huge against the tides

galactic gallop leading darkness
to its flourish

45: Directed by Desire

indivisible the vision sounding
space enough

enough

affinity and I am
where we want to be

particular and chronic

1969

THE WEDDING

Tyrone married her this afternoon
not smiling as he took the aisle
and her slightly rough hand.
Dizzella listened to the minister
staring at his wrist and twice
forgetting her name:
Do you promise to obey?
Will you honor humility and love
as poor as you are?
Tyrone stood small but next
to her person
trembling. Tyrone stood
straight and bony
black alone with one key
in his pocket.
By marrying today
they made themselves a man
and woman
answered friends or unknown
curious about the Cadillacs
displayed in front of Beaulah Baptist.
Beaulah Baptist
life in general

indifferent
barely known
nor caring to consider
the earlywed Tyrone
and his Dizzella
brave enough
but only two.

1967

THE RECEPTION

Doretha wore the short blue lace last night
and William watched her drinking so she fight
with him in flying collar slim-jim orange
tie and alligator belt below the navel pants uptight

"I flirt. You hear me? Yes I flirt.
Been on my pretty knees all week
to clean the rich white downtown dirt
the greedy garbage money reek.

I flirt. Damned right. You look at me."
But William watched her carefully
his mustache shaky she could see
him jealous, "which is how he always be

at parties." Clementine and Wilhelmina
looked at trouble in the light blue lace
and held to George while Roosevelt Senior
circled by the yella high and bitterly light blue face

he liked because she worked
the crowded room like clay like molding men
from dust to muscle jerked
and arms and shoulders moving when

she moved. The Lord Almighty Seagrams bless
Doretha in her short blue dress
and Roosevelt waiting for his chance:
a true gut-funky blues to make her really dance.

1967

LET ME LIVE WITH MARRIAGE

Let me live with marriage
as unruly as alive
or else alone and longing
not too long alone.
Love if unduly held by guilt
is guilty with fear
wronging that fixed impulse
to seek and ever more
to bind with love. Oh yes!
I am black within
as is this skin
without one pore
to bleed a pale defense: Will you attack
as cruel
as you claim me cruel? With word with silence
I have flung myself from you. And now
absurd
I sing of stillborn lyrics almost sung.

If this be baffling then the error's proved
To love so long and leave my love unmoved.

1965

THEN IT WAS

Then it was
our eyes locked slowly
on the pebble wash
of humus leaves and
peeled the plummet belly
of a thundercloud

You bent your neck
beneath a branch my
arms enclosed
and slipped your shadow
over me

Soon we had bathed
the sun fell at our feet
and broke into the sliding
ferment of our warmth

we were an early evening

1955

SAN JUAN

Accidental far into the longer light
or smoking
clouds that lip whole hillsides
spoken nearly foliated full
a free green ravelling alive
as blue as pale
as rectilinear

the red the eyebrow
covering a privacy a space
particular ensnarement
flowering roulette

49: Directed by Desire

place opening knees night water

color the engine air
on Sunday
silhouette the sound

and silently

some miles away the mountain
the moon
the same

1968

NOT LOOKING

Not looking now and then I find you here
not knowing where you are.
Talk to me. Tell me the things I see
fill the table between us or surround
the precipice nobody dares to forget.
Talking takes time takes everything
sooner than I can forget the precipice
and speak to your being there
where I hear you move no nearer
than you were standing on my hands
covered my eyes dreaming about music.

1967

WHEN I OR ELSE

when I or else when you
and I or we
deliberate I lose I
cannot choose if you if
we then near or where
unless I stand as loser
of that losing possibility
that something that I have
or always want more than much
more at
least to have as less and
yes directed by desire

1969

WHAT DECLARATION

What declaration can I make to clear
this room of strangers leaving
quickly as an enemy might come?
You look at me not knowing
I must guess what question I can ask
to open every mouth (and mine)
to free the throat (and yours) from fear.
We keep unknown to us
and I apart from me will search
my own deliberation my own you
and you and you, my own.

1967

51: Directed by Desire

MY SADNESS SITS AROUND ME

My sadness sits around me
    not on haunches not in any
    placement near a move
and the tired rolling
of a boredom without grief

If there were war
I would watch the hunting
I would chase the dogs
and blow the horn
because blood is commonplace

As I walk in peace
    unencountered unmolested
    unimpinging unbelieving unrevealing
    undesired under every O
My sadness sits around me

1965

ON YOUR LOVE

Beloved
where I have been
if
you loved me more than your own
and God's
soul
you could not have lifted me
out of the water
or
lit even one of the cigarettes I stood
smoking alone.

52: Things That I Do in the Dark

Beloved
what I have done
if
you discounted the devil
entirely
and rejected the truth as a rumor
you
would turn from the heat of my face
that burns
under your lips.

Beloved
what I have dreamed
if
you ended the fevers and riot
the claw and the wail and the absolute
furious
dishevel of my unkempt mind
you
could never believe the quiet
your arms
make true around me.

In your love I am sometimes redeemed
a stranger
to myself.

1971

ROMAN POEM NUMBER TWO

Toward the end of twenty minutes
we come to a still standing archway
in the city dump
nearby the motorcycle the treetrunk garbage
on the heavy smelling ground

as laurel bay leaves
(grecian laurel) break into

a heavy smell

Nicholas and Florence sharp last night
in life without an urban crisis that be-
longs to you

no demon in the throat of them
but sometimes just a harping on
the silence

No.

"What do you mean, *the subject*? That
has nothing to do with it."

"Listen I teethed on the Brooklyn Bridge"
she will insist her

refugee brown eyes and
hair showing artificial yellow

One can see how color is particularly hard
to manage in a personal way.

"I know every lamppost," she goes on.

Her husband adds another ending
to the movie we
Americans watched in American English
smack in the middle of this wonderful
Italian little Italian slum

"Let's put your money in the bank
—the retarded movie hero—he
would have been smiling at the heroine.
And that would have been," her husband continues
he repeats himself, "That would have been
a wonderful ending."

At this point his wife interrupts his
improvisation.

At the next evening table over espresso

the young woman married to a
well-educated employee
a first-rate worker in the First
National Bank Abroad

exclaims

"I have spent 3 days by myself!
Can you imagine?"

II

On that day exactly when
Christ was born
where the children sprawl and laugh out loud
where the disappearing churchclock only
bells from twelve to two
where I could break my cup of coffee
throwing wakeup at the knowing nuns
where we sit so close we see
each other sideways

the cobblestones turned black
with holy oil

but now ten lire
would be hard to find

and some of us seem
lost

1970

ROMAN POEM NUMBER EIGHT

He ordered a beer
She ordered a beer
I asked for apricot
yoghurt

55: Directed by Desire

"You know this game?
Nothing personal. For instance
June is all bird
but you," he spoke
to my rival, "You
are half-horse-half-
butterfly."
                    "Why
do you say I'm a bird?"

"Always up in the head
thinking
far from the earth."

I had been counting
the hairs on his wrist
but today
since he has been really
riding his horse
I venture to startle
the hairs of his arm
and listen to the thick
crackling
of his
persistent sex.

1970

ROMAN POEM NUMBER NINE

Return is not a way of going forward
after all
or back. In any case it seems
a matter of opinion how
you face although
the changing bed the different voice
around the different room

may testify to movement
entry exit it
is motion takes you in
and memory that lets you out again.
Or
as my love will let me say
the body travels faster than the keeping
heart will turn away.

1971

ROMAN POEM NUMBER TEN

Quarter past midnight and the sea
the dark blue music
does not belong to me

an elephant desire
heavy speeding whisper phantom
elephantom atmosphere

the heart rip hurts me
like the let go at the cliff

fell down shallow
loose and cold

let go
let go

1971

ROMAN POEM NUMBER ELEVEN

Spring has not arrived
and we already share
a beach that is a bed
where I can reach the worry
of his sometimes staring light blue
sometimes indecipherable
head
      (To reach is not to know
      or solve.
      A bed is not a beach
      exactly
      but the elements lie down the same.)
Outside
the cold and golden air
will strip my holding legs
bare on the back of his own red
motorcycle
but
I am warm my
arms my body most remember
from the night before
free
igneous
and he is there
between the memories
to take me.

1971

ROMAN POEM NUMBER THIRTEEN
For Eddie

Only our hearts will argue hard
against the small lights letting in the news
and who can choose between the worst possibility
and the last
between the winners of the wars against the breathing
and the last
war everyone will lose
and who can choose between the dry gas
domination of the future
and the past
between the consequences of the killers
and the past
of all the killing? There
is no choice in these.
Your voice
breaks very close to me my love.

1971

ROMAN POEM NUMBER FOURTEEN

believe it love
believe

      my lover
lying down he
lifts me up and high
and I am
high on him

believe it love
believe

the carnage scores around
the corner

59: Directed by Desire

o believe it love
believe

the bleeding fills the carnage cup
my lover lifts me
I am up
          and love is lying down

believe
believe it

crazies wear a clean shirt to the fire
o my lover
lift me higher higher

crazies take a scream and
make a speech they talk and
wash their mouths in dirt
no love will hurt
me lover lift me lying down

believe
believe it
carnage crazies
snap smash more more
(what you waiting for?)

you own the rope knife rifles the whole list
the searing bomb starch brighteners
the nuclear family whiteners

look the bridge be fallen down
look the ashes from the bones turn brown
look the mushroom hides the town
look the general wears his drip dry red
drip gown

o my lover nakedly
believe my love

believe
believe it

1971

60: Things That I Do in the Dark

ROMAN POEM NUMBER FIFTEEN
For Greg

Palm Sunday

(we)
duck underneath umbrellas
covering a snug an ugly
light of the wonderdreadful
faces that the watering streets
the concrete textures of transition
literal to rain like faulty colors
strip away
to livid blameful coloring
a wet a temporary
ransack through the earlier
when the rain started up so
unreasonable like one
child as the whole house
atmosphere
the separate bodies
separated
dry when no one will
try
the umbrella
no one will try
anything
anymore

1971

WEST COAST EPISODE

Eddie hung a light globe with the best electric
tape
he could find in
five minutes

then he left the room where he lives

to meet me

        (in Los Angeles)

Meanwhile the light globe fell and
smashed glass everywhere

        (the waterbed
        was dangerous
        for days)

but we used the paper bag that hid
the dollar-twenty-nine-California-Champagne
to hide
the light bulb
with a warm brown atmosphere

and that
worked really well

so there was no problem
except
we had to walk like feet
on broken seashells
even though
the color of the rug was green
and out beyond the one room
of our love
the world was mostly
dry.

                    1972

ON THE BLACK POET
READING HIS POEMS IN THE PARK
For Clarence and Sharyn

knit together firm a short triangular
full body holding lust but
tender then the words
grope wild to ask
around the woman
he loves do you
hear me am I
yours am
I

so he sounds uncertain
and the night-time
questions of his
poetry compel
the answers
from her
heart
that

comes and comes and comes and comes

1972

SHORTSONG FROM MY HEART

Within our love the world
looks like a reasonable easy plan
the continents the oceans
are not harder/larger than the dreams
our dreams
so readily embrace
and time is absolute newspace
beginning where you are

63: Directed by Desire

the sex of family and clear
far goal at once
beginning where you are
I am beginning to belong/be free
Let me be borne into the mystery
with you
Let me come home

1972

FOR MY BROTHER

Teach me to sing
Blackman Blacklove
sing when the cops break your head
full of song
sing when the bullets explode in the back
you bend over me
Blacklove Blackman
sing when you empty the world
to fill up the needles that kill
needles killing you
killing
you
teach me to sing
Blackman Blacklove
teach me to sing.

1972

ONESIDED DIALOG

OK. So she got back the baby
but what happened to the record player?

No shit. The authorized appropriation
contradicts my falling out of love?

You're wrong. It's not that I gave away my keys.
The problem is nobody wants to steal me or my house.

1972

POEM FOR MY PRETTY MAN

the complexity is like your legs
around me
simple
an entanglement
and strong
the ready
curling
hair
the brownskin tones of action
quiet
temporarily
like listening
serene
and passionate
and
slowly closer
slowly
closer
kissing

inch by inch

1973

65: Directed by Desire

IT'S ABOUT YOU:
ON THE BEACH

You have
two hands absolutely lean and clean
to let go the gold
the silver flat or plain rock
sand
but hold the purple pieces
atom articles
that glorify a color
yours is orange
oranges are like you love
a promising
a calm skin and a juice
inside
a juice
a running from the desert
Lord
see how you run
YOUR BODY IS A LONG BLACK WING
YOUR BODY IS A LONG BLACK WING

1972

ON THE PARADOX IN RHYME

When he comes on top of me
I am high as I can be.

1973

ABOUT THE REUNION

"I am rarely vindictive but
this summer I have taken great
pleasure in killing mosquitoes"

He says that to me
It is quite dark where we sit
and difficult to see

or tells me of work he will do
films of no end no beginning
and pours more wine
or takes another cigarette

And I know that is probably true
of his life of our love not to begin
not to end not be ugly or fine

But there is this history of once
when his hands and the length of his legs
came suddenly
to claim me all
bone and all flesh forcing away
the wall and the image of the wall
in one
fast meeting of amazement

And that was another year and somewhere
else

Here we talk outside
or do not talk

almost asleep in separated
wood chairs as hard as the time
between us
and
I admit
you are not as tall as the trees around me
your eyes are not as open as surprising
as the sea

but I watch for your words any changing
of your head
from a deadspot in the darkness
to a face

and finally you move

"I have to get in touch with
some other people"
you say
after so much silence

and I do not move

and
you leave.

1973

OF NIGHTSONG AND FLIGHT

There are things lovely and dangerous still

the rain
when the heat of an evening
sweetens the darkness with mist

and the eyes cannot see what the memory will
of new pain

when the headlights deceive
like the windows wild birds believe to be air
and bash bodies and wings
on the glass

when the headlights show space
but the house and the room and the bed and your face
are still there

68: *Things That I Do in the Dark*

while I am mistaken
and try to drive by

the actual kiss
of the world everywhere

1971

AFTER ALL IS SAID AND DONE

Maybe you thought I would forget
about the sunrise
how the moon stayed in the morning
time a lower lip
your partly open partly spoken
mouth

Maybe you thought I would exaggerate
the fire of the stars
the fire of the wet wood burning by
the waterside
the fire of the fuck the sudden move
you made me make
to meet you
(fire)

BABY
I do not exaggerate and
if
I could
I would.

1972

ABOUT LONG DISTANCES ON SATURDAY

he calls me from his house and
the timing seems bad
and I offer to call him back
later
but he says "no"
I'm about to split for the weekend
so
call me yeah
early next week or
sometime
and the answer is
that the question
is

(isn't it)

where are you going
baby

without me?

1972

POEM FOR MY LOVE

How do we come to be here next to each other
in the night
Where are the stars that show us to our love
inevitable
Outside the leaves flame usual in darkness
and the rain
falls cool and blessed on the holy flesh
the black men waiting on the corner for
a womanly mirage
I am amazed by peace
It is this possibility of you
asleep
and breathing in the quiet air

1972

ON MY HAPPY/MATRIMONIAL CONDITION

last time I got married was
yesterday (in
bed)
we stayed there
talking it over
nobody
shook
hands
but
the agreement
felt
very good
as a matter of fact
so
that was what
will be
the absolute
last time I ever
get
married

1973

CALLING ON ALL SILENT MINORITIES

HEY

C'MON
COME OUT

WHEREVER YOU ARE

WE NEED TO HAVE THIS MEETING
AT THIS TREE

AIN' EVEN BEEN
PLANTED
YET

1973

71: *Directed by Desire*

NO POEM BECAUSE TIME IS NOT A NAME

But beyond the
anxiety
the
querulous and reckless intersecting
conflict
and the trivial misleading banal
and separating fences every scrim
disguise each mask and feint
red herrings broadside poor
maneuvers of the
begging
hopeful
heart that wants and waits the
head that works against the minute
minute
There are pictures/memories of
temperature or cast or tone
or hue and vision
pictures of a dream
and dreams of memories and
dreams of gardens dreams of film
and pictures
of the daring
simple
fabulous
bold
difficult
and distant
inextricable
main
nigger
that I love
and
this is not
a poem

1972

ON A NEW YEAR'S EVE

Infinity doesn't interest me

not altogether
anymore

I crawl and kneel and grub about
I beg and listen for

what can go away

                    (as easily as love)

or perish
like the children
running
hard on oneway streets/infinity
doesn't interest me

not anymore

not even
repetition your/my/eye-
lid or the colorings of sunrise
or all the sky excitement
added up

is not enough

to satisfy this lusting adulation that I feel
for
your brown arm before it
moves

MOVES
CHANGES UP

the temporary sacred
tales ago
first bikeride round the house
when you first saw a squat
opossum
carry babies on her back

73: Directed by Desire

opossum up
in the persimmon tree
you reeling toward
that natural
first
absurdity
with so much wonder still
it shakes your voice

                    the temporary is the sacred
                    takes me out

and even the stars and even the snow and even
the rain
do not amount to much
unless these things submit to some disturbance
some derangement such
as when I yield myself/belonging
to your unmistaken
body

and let the powerful lock up the canyon/mountain
peaks the
hidden rivers/waterfalls the
deepdown minerals/the coalfields/goldfields/
diamond mines close by the whoring ore
hot
at the center of the earth

spinning fast as numbers
I cannot imagine

let the world blot
obliterate remove so-
called
magnificence
so-called
almighty/fathomless and everlasting
treasures/
wealth
(whatever that may be)

74: *Things That I Do in the Dark*

it is this time
that matters

it is this history
I care about

the one we make together
awkward
inconsistent
as a lame cat on the loose
or quick as kids freed by the bell
or else as strictly
once
as only life must mean
a once upon a time

I have rejected propaganda teaching me
about the beautiful
the truly rare

(supposedly
the soft push of the ocean at the hushpoint of the shore
supposedly
the soft push of the ocean at the hushpoint of the shore
is beautiful
for instance)
but
the truly rare can stay out there

I have rejected that
abstraction that enormity
unless I see a dog walk on the beach/
a bird seize sandflies
or yourself
approach me
laughing out a sound to spoil
the pretty picture
make an uncontrolled
heartbeating memory
instead

75: Directed by Desire

I read the papers preaching on
that oil and oxygen
that redwoods and the evergreens
that trees the waters and the atmosphere
compile a final listing of the world in
short supply

but all alive and all the lives
persist perpetual
in jeopardy
persist
as scarce as every one of us
as difficult to find
or keep
as irreplaceable
as frail
as every one of us

and
as I watch your arm/your
brown arm
just
before it moves

I know

all things are dear
that disappear

*all things are dear
that disappear*

1973

SUNFLOWER SONNET NUMBER ONE

But if I tell you how my heart swings wide
enough to motivate flirtations with the trees
or how the happiness of passion freaks inside
me, will you then believe the faithful, yearning freeze
on random, fast explosions that I place
upon my lust? Or must I say the streets are bare
unless it is your door I face
unless they are your eyes that, rare
as tulips on a cold night, trick my mind
to oranges and yellow flames around a seed
as deep as anyone may find
in magic? What do you need?

I'll give you that, I hope, and more
But don't you be the one to choose me: poor.

1975

SUNFLOWER SONNET NUMBER TWO

Supposing we could just go on and on as two
voracious in the days apart as well as when
we side by side (the many ways we do
that) well! I would consider then
perfection possible, or else worthwhile
to think about. Which is to say
I guess the costs of long term tend to pile
up, block and complicate, erase away
the accidental, temporary, near
thing/pulsebeat promises one makes
because the chance, the easy new, is there
in front of you. But still, perfection takes
some sacrifice of falling stars for rare.
And there are stars, but none of you, to spare.

1975

LULLABY

as suddenly as love

the evening burns a low
red
line occasional with golden glass
across the sky

i celebrate the color of the heat
you fill me with
the bloodbeat
you instill me with

as suddenly as love

1973

FOR ETHELBERT

if I cda known youd be real
back in them supreme court
gonna rule all evil out
days
I wda rushd to judgment
(lordy lord)
rushd thru
to the fiery seat itselve
and stayd there
cool as any momma madeup
her holy/everlastin min'
(chile *honey*!)
and sed
"sentence me, please,
to a long life long
enough
so's I gets to meet
what's comin afta (this mess)"
meanin'
you

1976

YOU CAME WITH SHELLS

You came with shells. And left them:
shells.
They lay beautiful on the table.
Now they lie on my desk
peculiar
extraordinary under 60 watts.

This morning I disturb I destroy the window
(and its light) by moving my feet
in the water. There.
It's gone.
Last night the moon ranged from the left
to the right side
of the windshield. Only white lines
on a road strike me as
reasonable but
nevertheless and too often
we slow down for the fog.

I was going to say a natural environment
means this or
I was going to say we remain out of our
element or
sometimes you can get away completely
but the shells
will tell about the howling
and the loss

1976

ON THE ALUMINUM

on the aluminum shelf
The Religious Experience of Mankind
would slide into a pile of sweet
pickles
except for the glassplate
that separates the two
elu-
sively

upright and sleepy in this depart-
mental armchair
I can see the light surprise
or titillate the still naked trees
and then
your eyes
(My God, the darkness of the sky
  around the stars
  moves like the sea
  incessantly)

love seems a matter of coincidence
at odds with the ending
of anyone/any two
                        at war with the boundaries
implied by
"i love you"

1976

MINUTES FROM THE MEETING

Some would rather know volcanoes
rumble with roulette like
lava lastingly
compelled
to hot or cold
deliverance

Some would rather know the rules
be miserable but safe
a well-dressed certainty
that runs from rain
and other
unbid
possibilities

But as for me
who knows no one to claim
her or propose
a scanning of the universe
or excavations
of a kiss

it is all
out of my arms

1976

QUEEN ANNE'S LACE

Unseemly as a marvelous an astral renegade
now luminous and startling (rakish)
at the top of its thin/ordinary stem
the flower overpowers or outstares me
as I walk by thinking *weeds* and *poison
ivy*, *bush* and *fern* or *runaway grass*:

81: Directed by Desire

You (where are you, really?) never leave me
to my boredom: numb as I might like to be.
Repeatedly
you do revive
arouse alive

a suffering.

1976

WASTED

You should slice the lying tongue of your love
into a billion bits of bile you swallow
one bilious element at a time
while
scalding water trembles drop
by drop between
(you hope)
between your eyes because
you said you loved me
and you lied
you lied

All you wanted was to rid me of my pride
to ruin me for tenderness
you lied
to thrust me monstrous from the hurt
you fabricated claiming
all the opposites of pain
while maiming
me
the victim of your whimsical disdain

And I still love you like the river
in the rain
in vain
you lied
in vain.

1976

FOR DAVE: 1976

There wasn't any hot water for the teapot
so you came by to fix the furnace
and you found me
"very pretty" (you said)
underneath my worries

Leaving the wind behind the door you came
and when you left to sleep elsewhere
you left me ready to keep on
dancing by myself

I was accustomed to the Army cap that spills your
hair below those clean-as-a-whistle ears nobody
knows how to blow so you can hear them honest-to-
God
But I was a stranger to your hair let free your arms
around me
reading my lips then licking them gentle as a bear
sure that he hugs a honey tree not going anywhere
(which is true: for you
                                        washing up with Ajax
leaving the rifle outside the way the Japanese
leave shoes
catching eels to smoke them good enough to eat
rebuilding a friend's house "after work")

Now you were lifting me as easily as we could laugh
between ourselves
you wanting to know what I was thinking about
me wanting to tell but unwilling to shout
at you (so you could hear me)

You arrive (red shirt
                    new shoes
                    the shower shining everywhere about you)
And I accept again
that there are simple ways of being joined

83: Directed by Desire

to someone
absolutely different from myself
And I admire the forthright
crocus first to mitigate the winter
with its thrust voluptuous/
on time

I mean to say
that it's not talk that brings us close together
and
thank god!

1976

METARHETORIC

Homophobia
racism
self-definition
revolutionary struggle

the subject tonight for
public discussion is
our love

we sit apart
apparently at oposite ends of a line
and I feel the distance
between my eyes
between my legs
a dry
dust topography of our separation

In the meantime people
dispute the probabilities
of union

They reminisce about the chasmic histories
no ideology yet dares to surmount

I disagree with you
You disagree with me
The problem seems to be a matter of scale

Can you give me the statistical dimensions
of your mouth on my mouth
your breasts resting on my own?

I believe the agenda involves
several inches (at least)
of coincidence and endless recovery

My hope is that our lives will declare
this meeting
open

1976

AGAINST THE
STILLWATERS

NOWADAYS THE HEROES

Nowadays the heroes go out looking
for the cradle in the cold
explore
a cemetery for beginnings
(irony can kill
                    the children panic at
the research in the glowing graveyard
what
what about
what about humanity in heat
the arms
the sleep alive?)
                    Look.
Look for the life
Look for reflections of the living
real problem:
money is the sun that makes us shine.

1970

47,000 WINDOWS

*The Lower East Side of New York City offers, in itself, a
history of American contradiction, devotion to profit, and the
failure of environmental design for human life. People had to
pass a law in order that ventilation and minimal, natural light
be available to the immigrants who had no money for decent
housing. Instead of tearing down the tenements that were
unfit for human habitation when they were first erected, the
reformers satisfied themselves by legislating phony windows
blasted into the bricks. That was a hundred years ago. Peo-
ple still have to live in those Lower East Side hellholes. This
is a poem about the law that passed some light and air into
that deliberated slum.*

1. There were probably more Indians alive
   than Jews and Italians in that whole
   early American place of New York
   when the city began being big:
   a perfect convergency confirmed
   congested with trade
   creating tolerance for trade requires
   abject curiosity or general indifference
   to anything that sells not well enough
   to tell somebody else about it. And
   at the beginning of New York
   the world was selling well and so was
   tolerance along with trade that
   provocation to a polyethnic population
   trading every bit of time for money
   made the city made me take
   your eye for mine according to extreme
   prosperity and appetite

2. In 1830 then the blurring crowd
   that overwhelming beggarly blur of people came
   they pushed into the seaport cornucopia of New York
   small many people forced
   from land from farms from food from family forced
   small many people left their universe inherited
   like seasons dictatorial
   the people fled
   political hostilities and hunger
   people fled
   that soon consuming triumph
   of elimination
   that machinery for triumph
   by a few

3. Then in 1830 the Astors and the Vanderbilts left.
   They rode by carriage from the uproar
   trouble from arrival by the millions
   shoved their ships that wandered
   with the sea to make their glad delivery

of travelers penniless and hellbent toward
the welcoming coast of always America

Those other ones
they came
not trading things
but lives.

4. Unskilled millions crammed old mansions
    broke apart large rooms and took a corner
    held a place a spot a bed a chair a box
    a looking glass
    and kept that space (except for death)
    a safety now for fugitives
    from infamy and famine
    working hard to live.

5. In place of land that street the outhouse
    tenement testimonies
    to a horrifying speculation that would quarter
    and condemn
    debase and shadow and efface
    the privacies of human being

6. Real estate arose as profit spread
    to mutilate the multitudes and kill them
    living just to live.
    What can a man survive?
    They say: The poor persist.

7. O the Chinese and the Irish and the names!
    The names survived.
    Likewise some families.

8. 1867 after the first and only Civil War
    men looked at others
    men again
    not targets.
    Looked at latrines six stories high
    people paralyzed by penury immobilized
    and children docked

and hopes untied and
lying loose and less than skeleton
at the dirty waters
by the building of a dollarbill
venality
near to nothing
at the doorway nothing
only life and speculation:
What can a man survive?

9. Men looked at other men again
   not targets
   and in 1869 they passed a law
   about the nightmare rising as they saw
   sick men and women nurse their babies
   although love
   is not enough to eat.

10. The Tenement Act of 1869
    was merciful, well-meant, and fine
    in its enforcement
    tore 47,000 windows out of hellhole
    shelter of no light.

    It must be hard to make a window.

1967

ON THE TWENTY-FIFTH ANNIVERSARY OF THE UNITED NATIONS: 1970

I

Of the world so beautiful the men and women
easy like the waters interchange and changing
make for change for children

An ordinary struggle through the day ignores
the natural tide below the waking crust

the one and simple earth before the breaking
of the waters
birth or separation from an early
urgent trust a solid continental
walkland for the one and simple walking
life

And yet we do go on

There are ways to count the trees
before they fall
and death is not the time for ceremony.
All before the end is all.

II

Light is history in flames.
Let us forget about the light.
Can anyone define
the darkness that defines the star?
We need to know about the darkness where
dreams go and where we are.

III

In the universe of many names love
fails like silence when the word is
love.
And like the first the onward screaming
of the witness
human soul will only listen when
the witness takes a stand.

1970

MAY 1, 1970

My Fellow Eggs and Apples
rising acid
from the rotten barrel belly
of the drunken killer whale

Here am I
a darkspot on
the underwear of ivory snow

Buggered by
this tricky mildew problem

How to clean out Mr. Clean
(I mean
Macbeth among the cherry blossoms)

Out!
The Moral laxative is working.
Quick! Fresh air! Fresh air!

We must prepare
for Operation Total Victory

Step One

Shave and a haircut FREE
for Miss America

1970

ON THE LOSS OF ENERGY
(and other things)

no more the chicken and the egg come

one of them
before the other

93: Against the Stillwaters

both
be fadin (steady)
from the supersafeway/a & p/giant
circus

> uh-huh
> the pilgrim cornucopia
> it ain' a pot to pee in
> much
> (these days)

gas is gone
and alka seltza runnin gas
a close race
outasight/you
name it
> toilet paper
> halfway honest politicians
there's a shortage
folks/*please*
step right up)
a crisis
(*come in closer*)
A International Disaster
Definitely Takin Place
(give the little lady down in front some room)
and (*how about the brother in the back row/can*
you hear me brother?)

> > WELL
> > I SAID THE HOT AIR'S RUNNIN
> > OUTASTEAM
> > I SAID
> > THE MEAT'S NOT GOOD
> > FOR KIDS TO EAT
> > TOO FULLAFAT
> > AND STUFF LIKE THAT
> > AND
> > IF YOU EAT MEAT
> > HOW YOU PLAN TO PAY THE
> > RENT?

94: Things That I Do in the Dark

I SAID
THE OILWELLS DRIBBLIN
LOWER THAN A SNAKE
AND SOON WON'T BE NO HEAT
AND SO YOU MIGHT AS WELL
   EAT MEAT
EXCEPT THERE AINT NO
MEAT TO EAT
I SAID

BROTHER CAN YOU SPARE A
DIME?

these things/they gettin more and more worse in
the time it takes to tell
you
how the country's bound to hell
you
first
if you be middlin poor or poor or Black or Black-and-poor
this profit-makin mess the worst
mess we been force to handle
since the civil war
close down the crackers
reconstructed
how the north won
into victory the crackers like to celebrate/a
reconstruction of the facts
on poor and Blackbacks
but
I am digressin/*folks*
please settle down and listen good
I say you know
you know
the affluent society
starvin high
on the hog as pigs can get
I say you know
we all been pigs
but mostly we been little pigs/I say

the big pigs
got the whole big pigpen
underneath some tasty big-pig pigs' feet
dynamite can move
where is the dynamite?
How come we tryin to cooperate
with this "emergency"/this faker/phony
ripoff
got you plannin
not to die and not to have a baby
on the weekends
not to do too much/
much less to start to die or start to have
a baby
on a Sunday
or on early Monday
got you/stiff and slow and hungry
on them lines the richboys laugh about/
Will somebody
real and prominent and smart
please stand
up here
and tell about inequities and big and little pigs
and other animals and birds/and fish
don't know a thing about no hog behavior/*where's
the dynamite?*
I say you know/I say
you know.
And so do I.

1974

FROM INSIDE THE CONTINUUM

well then let it all go
to hell
or wherever it may
But let the movement
in general
and mine
in particular
keep the pace of the days
in decision
       by tomorrow I will
       resolve to kill somebody
and what can I show
for this sumptuous proof
of consistency
       breathing in
       saying the names of things

hello
I am the victim who kills
I am the killer intending
to punish the past
for my destiny
       why
       does it require
       so much effort
       just to close the circle?

1975

97: Against the Stillwaters

AND WHO ARE YOU?

I

Leave my eyes
alone
why should I make
believe this place entirely

is white
and I am nothing

pasted to a fantasy
(big black phallus
wide white teeth)
of particles you
blast to pieces asking me
to swallow them as
monster bits

That bit is me.

and even if I wave my arms no
rule will stop the traffic
stop the hatred running near
with ropes and mongrels
on the mind blind cloth
and bloodhounds
at the cradle

II

Don't tell me windmills
like the color of maroon
which was OK
when I first saw a zebra

that's the color of her coat
and in the hallway where she
waits for money once a week

98: Things That I Do in the Dark

she pulls a spool
of silk along the needles

for a doily

don't tell me windmills
turn no more just
like the horse
that used to lead
the trolleys   you can't
help but smell four legs the
board above for two and hear him
bargaining to tune bananamato
peachpotato   awk   awk
parsley

nothing goes too fast

old fish and unwashed hair why
don't he cut the screwing get
him something nice   sits
on the step a
nylon stocking cap to
cover up his head the cat
fastidious outside
the room
of his secondhand bed

III

Old fish and unwashed hair
you may surmise by reading
the windows
bandaged with the Daily
News from World War
Two which anyway was not the first
that

nothing goes too fast

but slowly like the windmill
like the good milord

99: Against the Stillwaters

and Uncle Remus for a hero

O merrily the children
suffered verily the elevator
Boys with buttons
from the Army and the cleaning
Girls of fifty-five
                    "the children"
suffered as they came to
hear the wild and holy
black book out of the mouths
of the mob and underneath
a hanging tree

IV

Take the acolyte
obsequious and horsey
under lace

            on Monday

off the altar

on the stoop

and no more candles
in the vestibule a no
watt testicle just dangles

take the acolyte his
yellhello for girls his
little sister slow with shoes from '66
a blue harmonica inside her mouth o
sweetly play that Jesu Joy of
Man's Desiring and Desiring and desiring
she
should comb her hair at least or he
could screw forgiveness
for a change move
over but

don't tell me
drums and muscle

on the stoop

sit-in on the stoop
museum
tombstone of the horse maroon
dark dais insane sanctum
if you make it you play ball
                    talk loud
                    speak low
                    drink cheap
                    tell lies
                    LOOK AT THE PEOPLE

HE LOOKS LIKE A MAN
HE LOOKS LIKE ONE

1965

FOR BEAUTIFUL MARY BROWN:
CHICAGO RENT STRIKE LEADER

All of them are six
who wait inside that other room
where no man walks but many
talk about the many wars

Your baby holds your laboring arms
that bloat from pulling
up and down the stairs to tell
to call the neighbors: We can fight.

She listens to you and she sees
you crying on your knees or else
the dust drifts from your tongue and almost
she can feel her father standing tall.

101: Against the Stillwaters

Came to Chicago like flies to fish.
Found no heroes on the corner.
Butter the bread and cover the couch.
Save on money.

    Don't
tell me how you wash hope hurt and lose
don't tell me how you
sit still at the windowsill:

you will be god to bless you
Mary Brown.

            1965

OKAY "NEGROES"

Okay "Negroes"
American Negroes
looking for milk
crying out loud
in the nursery of freedomland:
the rides are rough.
Tell me where you got that image
of a male white mammy.
God is vague and he don't take no sides.
You think clean fingernails crossed legs a smile
shined shoes
a crucifix around your neck
good manners
no more noise
you think who's gonna give you something?

Come a little closer.
Where you from?

            1966

THE NEW PIETÀ: FOR THE MOTHERS AND CHILDREN OF DETROIT

They wait like darkness not becoming stars
long and early in a wrong one room
he moves no more

Weeping thins the mouth a poor escape from fire
lights to claim to torch the body
burial by war

She and her knees lock slowly closed (a burning door)
not to continue as they bled before
he moves no more

1965

WHAT WOULD I DO WHITE?

What would I do white?
What would I do clearly full
of not exactly beans nor
pearls my nose a manicure
my eyes a picture of your wall?

I would disturb the streets by
passing by so pretty kids
on stolen petty cash would look
at me like foreign
writing in the sky

I would forget my furs on any chair.
I would ignore the doormen at the knob
the social sanskrit of my life
unwilling to disclose my cosmetology,
I would forget.

Over my wine I would acquire
I would inspire big returns to equity

103: Against the Stillwaters

the equity of capital I am
accustomed to accept

like wintertime.

I would do nothing.
That would be enough.

1966

POEM FOR MY FAMILY: HAZEL GRIFFIN AND VICTOR HERNANDEZ CRUZ
Dedicated to Robert Penn Warren

I

December 15, 1811
a black, well-butchered slave
named George took leave of Old Kentucky—true
he left that living hell in pieces—
first his feet fell to the fire
and the jelly of his eyes lay smoking
on the pyre a long while—
but he burned complete
at last he left at least he got away.
The others had to stay there
where he died like meat
(that slave)

how did he live?

December 15, 1811

Lilburn Lewis and his brother
cut and killed somebody real
because they missed their mother:
Thomas Jefferson's sweet sister Lucy
Correction: Killed no body: killed a slave
the time was close to Christmas sent the poor

black bastard to the snow zones of a blue-eyed
heaven and he went the way he came like meat
not good enough to eat
not nice enough to see
not light enough to live
he came the way he went like meat.

                    POEM FOR 175 Pounds
                         ("Poor George")

II

Southern Kentucky, Memphis, New Orleans,
Little Rock, Milwaukee, Brooklyn, San Antonio,
Chicago, Augusta.
I am screaming
do you hear the pulse
destroying properties
of your defense against me and my life
now what are you counting
                         dollar bills or lives?
How did you put me down
as property?
as life?
How did you describe the damage?
I am naked
I am Harlem and Detroit
currently knives and bullets
I am lives
YOUR PROPERTY IS DYING
I am lives
MY LIFE IS BEING BORN
This is a lesson
in American History
What can you teach me?
The fire smells of slavery.

III

Here is my voice the speed and the wondering
darkness of my desire is
all that I am here
all that you never allowed:
I came and went like meat not good enough to eat
remember no remember
yes remember me
the shadow following your dreams
the human sound that never reached your ears
that disappear
vestigial
when the question is my scream
and I am screaming
whiteman
do you hear the loud
the blood, the real hysteria of birth
my life is being born
your property is dying

IV

What can you seize
from the furnace
what can you save?
America
I mean America how
do you intend to incinerate
my slavery?
I have taken my eyes from the light of your fires.
The begging body grows cold.
I see.
I see my self
Alive
A life

1967

FOR SOMEBODY TO START SINGING
(Song in Memory of Newark, New Jersey)

He's a man on the roof
on the run with a gun
he's a man

Boys and little girls
they were bad and they were good
now they're dead

He's a man on the roof
on the run with a gun
he's a man

Had no name and looked
the same but today
the soldiers tremble
at his aim

He's a man on the roof
on the run with a gun
he's a man

The country kept baiting
a people kept waiting
they all stood in line
then they left

He's a man on the roof
on the run with a gun
he's a man

If I have to kill myself
gone burn this box burn
all the locks
that keep me out

He's a man on the roof
on the run with a gun
he's a man

1967

LBJ: REJOINDER

The President talks about peril
to Negroes talking about power
and all I want to say
to him The President
(no less)
until we sway as many
people as he can scare
until we tell
and compel as loud and
as much as The Lonestar
State is large:
"Don't warn me Big
Buddy you have kept me
in my peril long enough you
been pushing Hush My Mouth on me
my lips been black and very blue
but nothing
else than now but power now
and nothing else
will warn
or worry you."

He lost the peace so
he can keep the peril he
knows war is nothing like please.

1967

IN MEMORIAM:
MARTIN LUTHER KING, JR.

I

honey people murder mercy U.S.A.
the milkland turn to monsters teach
to kill to violate pull down destroy

the weakly freedom growing fruit
from being born

America

tomorrow yesterday rip rape
exacerbate despoil disfigure
crazy running threat the
deadly thrall
appall belief dispel
the wildlife burn the breast
the onward tongue
the outward hand
deform the normal rainy
riot sunshine shelter wreck
of darkness derogate
delimit blank
explode deprive
assassinate and batten up
like bullets fatten up
the raving greed
reactivate a springtime
terrorizing

death by men by more
than you or I can

STOP

II

They sleep who know a regulated place
or pulse or tide or changing sky
according to some universal
stage direction obvious
like shorewashed shells

we share an afternoon of mourning
in between no next predictable
except for wild reversal hearse rehearsal
bleach the blacklong lunging

109: Against the Stillwaters

ritual of fright insanity and more
deplorable abortion
more and
more

1968

SOLIDARITY DAY, 1968

I

Down
between 2 monuments
the cameras and practically
balloons fried chicken cocktail
shrimp
a crayon poster megaphones
police

along the side as always
if you knew them
people

live like pigs

the children bruised and bare and brown
and big enough to know about a bitterness
from rats preoccupied
helpless competition

the fetter crazy male and female
blue green purple black revolving
slowly holy/brief
battalions limited to tear the entrails
clean like food
somebody grew

for garbage

II

american proximity a zebra

zoo the miserable journeymen
the jackass caravan

yeah yeah

show the sharks their carnage
look at that
humility in hunger

marks the moment of the mud

III

in the kitchen listening
a child sits at a table
steps away from basement stairs
his parents carry ashes
up
his parents rising from the cellar
hold on lug the heavy
heaving holdon lift
the buckets

carry through the ashes

IV

Resurrection died
but not like Jesus only
nailed and crucified

resurrection died
all during the rain
and right among the roses
and under wonderful trees

resurrection died
in full consideration of various

proposals here set forth
or there further considered
or in dedicated statements of nevertheless
never and no
in overweight in ties
in musical clock alarms
in uniform in limousines
in wellattended classrooms
and in ordinary church
from coast to coast

on holiday
on little more than grits
and other bits of boomerang bravado

resurrection went the way the money's spent
on *d, e, dash, dash, ashes.*

1968

NO TRAIN OF THOUGHT
(April 4, 1969)

A year runs long enough
from force momentum trips
the memory

hard dark tracks

rush hatred hearts
nobody destination
home away

parallels to scare the starting place
start
tracks together
hard dark real long bloody tracks

pull pointless

killers
kill people pointless
killing (people) life
killing (people) love
killing (people)

partly (   )

killing

all of us (   )

1969

I CELEBRATE THE SONS OF MALCOLM

I celebrate the sons of Malcolm
multiplying powerful
implicit
passionate and somber
              Celebrate
the sons of Malcolm gather
black unruly as alive and hard
against the papal skirts the palace
walls collapsing
              Celebrate
the sons of Malcolm hold my soul
alert to children building
temples on their feet to face the
suddenly phantom terrors
              Celebrate
the sons of Malcolm fathering the person
destinies arouse a royal yearning
culminate magnificent
and new

1969

CAMEO NO. I

Abraham Lincoln shit he never walked nowhere to read
a book tell all about it all about
the violation the continuous the fuck my face
the dark and evil dark is evil no good dark
the evil and continuous
the light the white the literature he read was
lying blood to leech the life away

believe the Abraham the Lincoln log the literature
the books he read the book he wrote down put
down
put you on the rawhide prairie
emancipated proclaiming
Illinois the noise
the boombang bothering my life
the crapcrashchaos print the words
the sprightly syllable destruction
nobody black black nobody black nobody
black
nobody

man

he no Abraham no kind
a president a power walk the miles and read the piles of
pages pale to murder real

                        no wonder he was so depressed

that character
cost me almost
my whole
future   times

                                                    1969

CAMEO NO. II

The name of this poem is

George Washington
somebody want me to think he bad

he bad

George Washington the father of this country
the most the first the holy-poly ghost
the father of this country
took my mother

anyway you want to take that

George the father hypocrite
his life some other bit
than freedom down to every man

George Washington he think he big
he trade my father for a pig

his ordinary
extraordinary human
slaves 300 people Black
and bleeding life beholden to the Presidential
owner underneath the powder of his wicked wig
he think he big

he pull a blackman from his pocket
put a pig inside the other one
George Washington

the father of this country
stocked
by declarations at the auction block

Prez Washington he say
"give me niggers
let me pay

by check"
(Check the father of this country
what he say:)

"I always pay for niggers
let them stay
like vermin
at Mount Vernon"

inpeccable in battle
ManKill Number One
the revolutionary head
aristocratic raider at the vulnerable
slavegirl bed

Americanus Rex
Secretus Blanco-Bronco-Night-Time-Sex

the father of this country
leading privileges of rape and run

George Washington

somebody tell me how he bad he big

I know how he
the great great great great
great great proto-

typical

1969

IN THE TIMES OF MY HEART

In the times of my heart
the children tell the clock
a hallelujah
          listen people
          listen

1969

MEMO TO DANIEL PRETTY MOYNIHAN

You done what you done
I do what I can

Don't you liberate me
from my female black pathology

I been working off my knees
I been drinking what I please

And when I vine
I know I'm fine
I mean
All right for each and every Friday night

But you been screwing me so long
I got a idea something's wrong
with you

I got a simple proposition
You takeover my position

Clean your own house, babyface.

1969

MAY 27, 1971: NO POEM

blood stains Union Street in Mississippi

so now there will be
another investigation to see
whether or not
the murder of the running young girl
by drunken whiteboys
was
a Federal offense
                    "of some kind"

there are no details to her early death
her
high school graduation
glory
yellow dress
branded
new the rolled-up
clean
diploma
certifying ready
certifying aim
certifying shot
by bathtub whiskey hatred by
a bloody .22 let loose
at her life

Joetha Collier she was
killed

at eighteen only
daughter
born to Mr. and to Mrs. Love
the family
Black love wracked
by outside hogstyle hatred
on the bullet fly

Joetha Collier she was
young and she
was Black and she was
she was
she was

and

blood stains Union Street in Mississippi

1971

ON THE MURDER OF TWO HUMAN BEING BLACK MEN, DENVER A. SMITH AND HIS UNIDENTIFIED BROTHER, AT SOUTHERN UNIVERSITY, BATON ROUGE, LOUISIANA, 1972

I

What you have to realize is about private property
like
for example do you know how much the president's
house weighs in at

do you know that?

But see it's important because obviously
that had to be some heavy building some kinda
heavy heavy bricks and whatnot
dig
the students stood outside the thing
outside of it
and also
on the grass belonging to somebody else (although
who the hell can tell who owns the grass)
but
well the governor/he said the students
in addition
to standing outside the building that was
The House of The President
in addition to that and in addition to
standing on the grass that was growing
beside that heavy real estate
in addition (the governor said) the students
used
quote vile language unquote and
what you have to realize about quote
vile language unquote
is what you have to realize about private property
and
that is

you and your mother and your father and your
sister and your brother
you
and you and you
be strictly lightstuff on them scales
be strictly human life
be lightstuff
weighing in at zero
plus
you better clean your language up

don't be be calling mothafuckas *mothafuckas*
pigs *pigs*
animals *animals*
murderers *murderers*
you
weighing less than blades of grass the last
dog peed on
less than bricks smeared grey by pigeon shit
less than euphemisms for a mercenary and
a killer
you be lightstuff
lightstuff on them scales

look out!

1972

FOR MICHAEL ANGELO THOMPSON
(October 25, 1959–March 23, 1973)

So Brooklyn has become a holy place

the streets have turned to meadowland
where
wild
free
ponies
eat among the wild
free
flowers
growing there

> Please do not forget.

A tiger does not fall or stumble
broken by an accident.
A tiger does not lose his stride or
clumsy
slip and slide to tragedy
that buzzards feast upon.

> Do not forget.

The Black prince Michael Black boy
our young brother
has not "died"
he
has not "passed away"

the Black prince Michael Black boy

our young brother

> He was killed.
> He did not die.

It was the city took him off
(that city bus)
and smashed him suddenly

121: Against the Stillwaters

to death
deliberate.

It was the city took him off
the hospital
that turned him down the hospital
that turned away from so much beauty
bleeding
bleeding
in Black struggle
                    just to live.
It was the city took him off
the casket names and faces
of the hatred spirit
stripped the force the
laughter and the agile power
of the child

                    He did not die.
                    A tiger does not fall.
                    Do not forget.

The streets have turned to meadowland
where
wild
free
ponies
eat among the wild
free
flowers
growing there

and Brooklyn
has become a holy place.

                                        1973

POEM AGAINST THE STATE
(OF THINGS): 1975

wherever I go (these
days)
the tide seems low
(oh) wherever I go (these
days)
the tide seems very
very low

ATTICA!
ALLENDE!
AMERIKA!

Welcome to the Sunday School
of outfront machineguns
and secretive
assassinations

EVERYBODY WELCOME!

Put your money on the plate
your feet on the floor
and better keep a bodyguard
standing at the open door

EVERYBODY WELCOME!

Almighty
Multinational
Corporate
Incorporeal
Bank of the World
The World Bank
Diplomacy
          and Gold

This is the story:
This is the prayer:

          Rain fell
          Monday the thirteenth

123: Against the Stillwaters

1971
Attica
coldstone covered by a cold moon-
light hidden by the night
when fifteen hundred Black
Puerto Rican
White (one or two)
altogether Fifteen Hundred Men
plus
thirty-eight hostages
(former keepers of the keys
to the ugliest
big
house of them all)
Fifteen Hundred and Thirty
Eight
Men
lay sleeping in a long
wait
for the sun
and not one with a gun
not one with a gun

(oh) wherever I go
the tide seems low

Fifteen Hundred and Thirty
Eight
prisoners in prison
at Attica/they
lay sleeping in a long
long wait
for the sun
and not one with a gun
not one with a gun

But they were not really alone:

ATTICA!
ALLENDE!
AMERIKA!

124: Things That I Do in the Dark

Despite
the quiet of the cold moon-
light on the coldstone
of the place
Despite
the rain that fell
transforming the D-yard
blankets and tents
into heavyweight, soggy
and sweltering hell

The Brothers were hardly alone:

on the roofs
on the walkways
in turrets
and tunnels
from windows
and whirlybirds

overhead

The State
Lay in wait

Attica Attack Troops
wearing masks
carrying gas cannisters
and proud to be white
proud to be doing
what everyone can
for The Man
Attica Attack Troops
lay armed
at the ready
legalized killers
hard
chewing gum
to master an all-American impatience
to kill
to spill blood
to spill blood of the Bloods

and not one with a gun

> the State
> lay in wait
>
> Attica Attack Troops
> carrying pistols and
> big-game/.270 rifles and
> Ithaca Model 37 shotguns
> with double-o buckshot
> and also
> shotguns appropriate
> for "antivehicle duty"
> or shotguns appropriate
> for "reducing a cement block wall
> to rubble"
> they were ready
>
> *for what?*

(oh) wherever I go (these
days)
the tide seems low

> Fifteen Hundred and Thirty Eight
> Prisoners
> lay waiting for the next
> day's sun
> Fifteen Hundred and Thirty Eight
> Brothers
> asleep
> and not one with a gun
> not one with a gun

II

Why did the Brothers revolt
against Attica?

> *why were they there?*

What did they want?

                    the minimum wage
                    less pork
                    fresh fruit
                    religious freedom
                    and more than one shower a week

What did they want?

                    a response
                    recognition
                    as men

                    "WE are MEN!" They
                     declared:
                    "WE are MEN!
                     We are not beasts and do not
                     intend to be beaten
                     or driven as such."

ATTICA!
ALLENDE!
AMERIKA!

                    The State
                    lay in wait.

III

Black woman weeping at the coldstone wall
Rain stops. And blood begins to fall

                    "JACKPOT ONE!" was the animal
                    cry of The State
                    in its final
                    reply
                            "JACKPOT ONE!!"
                    was the cry

                    9:26 A.M.
                    Monday the thirteenth
                    September, 1971
                    Police

State Troopers
prison guards
helicopters/The Attica Attack Troops
terrified the morning
broke through
to the beasts within them
beasts
unleashed by the Almighty
Multinational
Corporate
Incorporeal
Bank of the World
Despoilers
of Harlem
Cambodia
Chile
Detroit
the Phillipines
Oakland
Montgomery
Dallas
South Africa
Albany
Attica
Attica
The Attica Killers
The Almighty State shot/
murdered/massacred
forty three men
forty three men

The other Brothers/they
were gassed and
beaten
bleeding or not
still clubbed and beaten:

"Nigger! You should
  have got it through the head!

Nigger! You gone wish that you were
dead!   Nigger!   Nigger!"

Monday the Thirteenth
September, 1971
Attica
Blood fell on the Brothers: Not one with a gun.
Black women weeping into coldstone.

IV

> *wherever I go (these*
> *days)*
> *the tide seems low*
> *(oh) wherever I go (these*
> *days)*
> *the tide seems very*
> *very low*
>
> *God's love has turned away*
> *from this Almighty place*
> *But*
> *I will pray*
> *one prayer while He yet grants me*
> *time and space:*
>
> > NO MORE AND NEVER AGAIN!
> > NO MORE AND NEVER AGAIN!
>
> > A-men.
> > A-men.

1975

NEW LIKE NAGASAKI
NICE LIKE NICENE

Out of the marketplace where
would I go?
Even Holy Communion and I met
my Host across the counter
there in Brooklyn High
Episcopalian
incense of expensive rites
I bowed my braided hair
and held my head as low
as all the rules

I believe the bedside
manner of the church
within the temples full of
gold I believe the gold the
body and the blood let in my name
as citizen belonging to the marketplace
I believe the sale and take the credit
as it comes

Jesus Christ
or God
the creed expands as progress moves
along in step like soldiers
marching everywhere at once
the unsung partners of the great
big bigger biggest button
manufacturers
more buttons for the uniform
shroud paring of the profits from
the boys who wear the flags and
off-days flip their zippers to half-
mast the boys who
fly the planes that kill
the children
over there.

I believe the boys the planes the
button for the uniform the gory raiment
I believe that anyone can be a Christian
like a camera let's
reverse morality read right
to left what else
beside the marketplace what else?
Where would I go? And think about it:

Why would I know your name?

1966

EXERCISE IN QUITS
(November 15, 1969)

I

           moratorium means well what
you think it means you
dense? Stop it means stop.

We move and we march sing songs
move march sing songs move march move

It/stop means stop.

           hey mister man

how long you been fixing to kill somebody?
Waste of time
         the preparation training

you was born a bullet.

II

we be wondering what they gone do
all them others left and right
what they have in mind

131: Against the Stillwaters

about us
and who by the way is "us"

listen you got a match you got the light
you got two eyes two hands
why you taking pictures of the people
what you sposed to be you
got to photograph the people?

you afraid you will (otherwise) forget
what people look like?

man
or however you been paying dues

we look like you

                on second thought
there is a clear resemblance to the dead
among the living so

go ahead go on
and take my picture

quick

1969

LAST POEM FOR A LITTLE WHILE

I

Thanksgiving 1969
Dear God I thank you for the problems that are mine
and evidently mine alone

By mine I mean just ours
crooked perishable blue like blood
problems yielding to no powers
we can muster we can only starve or stud
the sky the soil the stomach of the human hewn

II

(I am in this crazy room
where people all over the place
look at people all over the place
For instance Emperors in Bronze Black Face
Or Buddha Bodhisattva sandstone trickled old and dirty into
    inexpensive, public space.)

Insanity goes back a long time I suppose.
An alien religion strikes me lightly
And I wonder if it shows
then how?

III

Immediately prior to the messed-up statues that inspire
monographs and fake mistakes
the Greco-Roman paraplegic tricks
the permanently unbent knee
that indoor amphitheater that celebrates the amputee—

Immediately prior to the messed-up statues
just before the lucratively mutilated choir
of worthless lying recollection

There the aged sit and sleep;
for them museum histories spread too far too deep
for actual exploration

(aged men and women) sit and sleep
before the costly exhibition can begin

to tire what remains of life.

IV

If love and sex were easier
we would choose something else
to suffer.

133: Against the Stillwaters

V

Holidays do loosen up the holocaust
the memories (sting tides) of rain and refuge
patterns hurt across the stranger city
holidays do loosen up the holocaust
They liberate the stolen totem tongue

The cripples fill the temple
palace entertainment under glass
the cripples crutching near the columns swayed
by plastic wrap
disfiguring haven halls or veils the void
impromptu void
where formerly
Egyptian sarcasucker or more recently
where European painting
turns out nothing
no one
I have ever known.

These environments these
artifacts facsimiles these
metaphors these
earrings vase that sword
none of it
none of it
is somehow what I own.

VI

Symbols like the bridge.
Like bridges generally.
Today a flag a red and white and blue new flag
confused the symbols in confusion
bridge over the river
flag over the bridge
The flag hung like a loincloth flicked in drag.

VII

Can't cross that bridge. You listen
things is pretty bad
you want to reach New Jersey
got to underslide the lying spangled banner.
Bad enough New Jersey.
Now Songmy.
Songmy. A sorrow song. Songmy.
The massacre of sorrow songs.
Songmy. Songmy. Vietnam.
Goddamn. Vietnam.
I would go pray about the bridge.
I would go pray a sorrow Songmy song.
But last time I looked the American flag was flying
from the center of the crucifix.

VIII

"Well, where you want to go?"
he asks. "I don't know. It's a long
walk to the subway."
"Well," he says, "there's nothing at home."
"That's a sure thing," she answers.
"That's a sure thing: Nothing's at home."

IX

Please pass the dark meat.
Turkey's one thing I can eat
and eat.
eeney eeney meeney mo
It's hard to know
whether I should head into
a movie
or take the highway to the airport.
Pass the salt.
Pass the white meat.

Pass the massacre.
o eeney eeney myney mo.
How bad was it, exactly?
What's your evidence?
Songmy o my sorrow
eeney meeney myney mo
Please pass the ham.
I want to show
Vietnam how we give thanks
around here.
Pass the ham.
And wipe your fingers on the flag.

X

Hang my haven
Jesus Christ
is temporarily off
the wall.

XI

American existence twists
you finally
into a separatist.

XII

I am spiders
on the ceiling of a shadow.

XIII

Daumier was not mistaken.
Old people sleep with their mouths open
and their hands closed flat
like an empty wallet.

So do I.

1969

REALIZING THAT REVOLUTION WILL
NOT TAKE PLACE BY TELEPHONE

I

It's morning. We get up old
and then
discovering the waters of the bay
changed
in the night towards a world of water
waves
whitecaps posing at the windows
wild
ducks beside both doors
swimming calmly
and the wind
smash rushing thrust push shaking
ancient tower trees the kitchen walls
our confidence
in staying
anywhere

(discovering the transformation
we moved slowly so
reluctant to transform ourselves
although
I guess my son could be an elegant
canoe
and I could try to be a dark blue
sail)

II

We thought we got up (old)
but we were different
in a sudden thoroughgoing difference
a highly irregular
a natural
storm

137: Against the Stillwaters

surrounded the table and the breakfast
was an absentminded
habit up against
the closing shock of danger
outdoors
racing nearer
raising water three to seven feet
of water free
great rhythms
                    racing nearer
high
over the whole flat marshland
                                        fish
came by amazed by drowning grass
and we

we called the Weather Bureau

III

They said we knew
the ocean and the bay the sky and
northeast blasting
45 to 60 mile per hour winds
beat non-stop breaking eardrums

They said

Good Morning
Weather Forecast for Nassau and Suffolk County
precipitation probability
barometer thermometer

warnings
flood

winds
heavy rains

They said
            GET OFF THE TELEPHONE

OVERNIGHT
ALL THINGS HAVE CHANGED
THE CHANGES ARE THE THINGS YOU KNOW.
THE WEATHER AND THE WORLD ARE WHERE
  YOU ARE.
TOMORROW MORNING
WHEN YOU WAKE UP
WILL
YOU WAKE UP?

PLEASE GET OFF THE PHONE!

1971

TO MY SISTER, ETHEL ENNIS, WHO SANG "THE STAR-SPANGLED BANNER" AT THE SECOND INAUGURATION OF RICHARD MILHOUS NIXON, JANUARY 20, 1973

gave proof through the night
that our flag was still there

on his 47th inauguration of the killer king
my sister
what is this song
you have chosen to sing?

and the rockets' red glare
the bombs bursting in air
my sister
what is your song to a flag?

to the twelve days of Christmas
bombing when the homicidal holiday shit tore forth
pouring from the b-52 bowels loose over Hanoi and the skin
and the agonized the blown limbs the blinded eyes the

139: Against the Stillwaters

silence of the children dead on the street and the
incinerated homes and Bach Mai Hospital blasted and
drowned by the military the American shit vomit
dropping down death and burying the lives the people
of the new burial ground
under the flag

for the second coronation of the killer king
what is this song
you have chosen to sing?

my sister
when will it come finally clear
in the rockets' red glare
my sister
after the ceremonial guns salute the ceremonial rifles
saluting the ceremonial cannons that burst forth a choking
smoke to celebrate murder
will it be clear
in that red that bloody red glare
my sister
that glare of murder and atrocity/atrocities
of power
strangling every program
to protect and feed and educate and heal and house
the people

(talking about *us*/you and me talking
about *us*)

when will it be clear to you

which night will curse out the stars with the blood
of the flag
for you
for enough of us

by the rockets' red glare
when will it be clear
that the flag that this flag is still there is still
here and will smother you smother your songs

140: Things That I Do in the Dark

can you see
my sister
is the night
and the red glaring blood clear at last
say

can you see
my sister

say you can see
my sister

and sing no more of war

1973

ON MORAL LEADERSHIP
AS A POLITICAL DILEMMA
(Watergate, 1973)

I don't know why but
I cannot tell a lie

I chopped down the cherry tree
I did
I did that
yessirree
I chopped down the cherry tree

and to tell you the truth
see
that was only in the morning

which left a whole day and part
of an evening (until suppertime)
to continue doing what I like to do

about cherry trees

which is

to chop them down

then pick the cherries
and roll them into a cherry-pie circle
and then
stomp the cherries
stomp them
jumping up and down

hard and heavy
jumping up to stomp them
so the flesh leaks and the juice
runs loose
and then I get to pick at the pits
or else I pick up the cherry pits
(depending on my mood)
and then
I fill my mouth completely full
of cherry pits
and run over to the river
the Potomac
where I spit
the cherry pits
47 to 65 cherry pits spit
into the Potomac
at one spit

and to tell you the truth some more
if I ever see a cherry tree
standing around no matter where
and here let me please be perfectly clear
no matter where
I see a cherry tree
standing around
even if it belongs to a middle-American of
moderate means with a two-car family
that is falling apart in a respectable

civilized
falling apart
mind-your-manners manner

even then

or even if you happen to be
corporate rich or
unspeakably poor or famous
or fashionably thin or comfortably fat
or even as peculiar as misguided as
a Democrat

or even a Democrat

even then
see
if you have a cherry tree
and I see it
I will chop that cherry tree down
stomp the cherries
fill my mouth completely with the pits to
spit them into the Potomac
and I don't know why
it is
that I cannot tell a lie

but that's the truth.

1973

UHURU IN THE O.R.

*The only successful heart transplant, of the first five attempts,
meant that a black heart kept alive a white man—a white
man who upheld apartheid.*

I like love anonymous
more than murder incorporated or
shall we say South Africa
I like the Valentine the heart the power
incorruptible but failing body
flowers of the world

From my death the white man
takes new breath he stands as
formerly he stood and he commands me
for his good he overlooks
my land my people
in transition transplantations
hearts   and power
beating beating beating beating
hearts in transplantation
power in transition

1965

I MUST BECOME A MENACE
TO MY ENEMIES
*Dedicated to the Poet Agostinho Neto,
President of The People's Republic of Angola: 1976*

I
I will no longer lightly walk behind
a one of you who fear me:
                              Be afraid.
I plan to give you reasons for your jumpy fits
and facial tics

I will not walk politely on the pavements anymore
and this is dedicated in particular
to those who hear my footsteps
or the insubstantial rattling of my grocery
cart
then turn around
see me
and hurry on
away from this impressive terror I must be:
I plan to blossom bloody on an afternoon
surrounded by my comrades singing
terrible revenge in merciless
accelerating
rhythms
But
I have watched a blind man studying his face.
I have set the table in the evening and sat down
to eat the news.
Regularly
I have gone to sleep.
There is no one to forgive me.
The dead do not give a damn.
I live like a lover
who drops her dime into the phone
just as the subway shakes into the station
wasting her message
cancelling the question of her call:

fulminating or forgetful but late
and always after the fact that could save or
condemn me

I must become the action of my fate.

II

How many of my brothers and my sisters
will they kill
before I teach myself
retaliation?

145: *Against the Stillwaters*

Shall we pick a number?
South Africa for instance:
do we agree that more than ten thousand
in less than a year but that less than
five thousand slaughtered in more than six
months will
WHAT IS THE MATTER WITH ME?

I must become a menace to my enemies.

III

And if I
if I ever let you slide
who should be extirpated from my universe
who should be cauterized from earth
completely
(lawandorder jerkoffs of the first the
  terrorist degree)
then let my body fail my soul
in its bedevilled lecheries

And if I
if I ever let love go
because the hatred and the whisperings
become a phantom dictate I o-
bey in lieu of impulse and realities
(the blossoming flamingos of my
  wild mimosa trees)
then let love freeze me
out.

I must become
I must become a menace to my enemies.

1976

FROM *THE TALKING BACK*
OF MISS VALENTINE JONES

THE WAR IS OVER:

And
the small fry
littlefolk
slant-eye devils
gooks
the fertile peril
yellow
fellow travellers

THEY'VE WON:

The victory
the liberation
of the Indo-Chinese peoples
apparently
belongs to pint-size
short
slight
runt-hard armies
not excluding ten-year-olds
boyandgirl
guerilla fireflies
a multi-thousandfold
an army
marching on and on
in .69¢
single-thong slippers
thin
loose pyjamas
a military presence
fortified
by a handful of rice
wild fruit
and the indomitable
sexy

instinct sexy sting
of freedom

                   (WANT THAT THING
                    THAT MIGHTY
                    SWEET THING SO MY SOUL
                    CAN SING
                    WANT FREEDOM
                            FREEDOM
                            FREEDOM
                    WANT MY FREEDOM
                    NOW)

                       *

There go the imperial
big-nose
eagles
      flown and blown
      BACK
      where they come from

LOOK AT 'EM GO:

      a-slippin and a-slidin
      a-tippin and a-hidin
      and hardly afloat
      and doin a desperate
      flip-floppin
      wing-down
      to the nearest Red Cross
      rescue boat

LOOK AT 'EM GO:

The imperial
big-nose
eagles
flying low enough to crawl

              crawl eagle crawl
              wipe your weepy eyes
              turn to the west my darlin
              fly the friendly skies

148: Things That I Do in the Dark

"LONG LISTANCE IS CHEAPER THAN YOU THINK"

LOOK AT 'EM GO!

THE WAR IS OVER!

*

In Xuan Loc
Hanoi
Phnom Penh
and Ho Chi Minh City
there are no
        people/babies/lovers/widows/**mothers**
        brothers/in-laws/children
        who belong to
        who survive
        who grieve for
        the crewcut losers of the war

the eagle-eye
anti-personnel missionaries
took no
        land/nation/village/school/hospital
        home/gardenplot
        or rice field
        with them
        when they split

However
authorities attribute
these remaining items
to the big-nose foreigners
                five pounds: ground round
                frozen orange juice
                a watch that runs under water
                filter tip cigarettes
                and a case of Coca-Cola

      and that's all
      think small
      THE WAR IS OVER

*

This myopic personage
pimply where she
wish she bloomin freckles
tell me

smack in the middle of the giant cock-
eyed suckers
truckin us into the ground
squeezin heads to the size of the sides
of a dime
smack then
when everybody hurt
for open/
free meals an'
open/
free schools an'
open/
free ways to a job
an'open/
free dreams of the future

when
the men
drink whiskey from brown bags
on the daylong corner places they don'
never leave
                  (o i need me somethin i can do
                   need me somethin i can do
                   well i have some kinda blues
                   well i have some kinda food
                   but it don' really taste too good)

Smack then and there
this myopic personage
she tells me

"They don't look like students!
They don't act like students!!
It drives me crazy.
They come

doo-wah-ooo-ooh
Oh-Oh-Ba-Bee
playing those Japanese portable
radios
loud
so you can't hear nothing
worthwhile
or think
or carry on a proper
conversation
or
(for Goddsake)
read a book! That's why I
say, honestly, Valentine,
we have only ourselves to
blame. Blackfolk got only
themselves to blame. You
don't see no white kids
carrying no radios.
Do you?"

I say,
"Maybe they don't have no radio."

My man,
Emanuel Addis Addaba Boo
Owens,
he say,
"Maybe they don't have no
need to dance through
streets of fire: Lady,
buy a radio!
Turn it up
turn it on
on and on/on and on
turn it up

don' wanna hear you
or be near you

151: Against the Stillwaters

you the problem
you the dryspot in the holy water
you the freezeass/imitation enemy

He say,
"Lady, buy a radio!"

＊ *(The Writings on the Wall)*

"Dear Somebody
    I am un-happy. My boy-
    friend is a creep. He
    makes me
    sick. What should I do?
    Nobody likes me be-
    sides him, either."

. . .

"You should talk
over with him how he's
a creep and tell him how
you feel about that. May-
be he thinks you're a creep, too.
How do you know? Find out."

. . .

"I am not a lesbian but
I would like to have a real
experience with a girl who
is. What should I do?"

. . .

"Believe it or not, Jesus
is the answer. Join the
church. The Lord will
save you a lot of
trouble and keep you
busy on the weekends."

. . .

"Boycott the Bicentennial"

. . .

"My man say if I don't give
him a baby
boy
he will throw me
out or beat
me to death."

                                    . . .

"Tell him to fuck himself.
Don't he like girls?"

                              *

I'm tellin you baby
the war's not hardly over
for anyone like me

We got a long way to go
before we get to where we need to be

Don' have no work
(don' have no work)
Can' fin' no job

The streets is mean
(the streets is mean)
An' my ship ain' nowhere
to be seen

The war's not hardly over
                    (WANT THAT THING
                     THAT MIGHTY
                     SWEET THING SO MY SOUL
                     CAN SING
                     WANT FREEDOM
                              FREEDOM
                              FREEDOM
                     WANT MY FREEDOM
                              NOW!

                        *

In Africa
in Mozambique

153: Against the Stillwaters

Angola
liberation lifts
the head of the young girl
formerly burdened by laundry
and yams

She
straps the baby to her back
and
she carries her rifle
like she means
means to kill

for the love

for the life
of us all

1976

TOWARDS
A PERSONAL
SEMANTICS

I AM UNTRUE YET I

That fool myself
at yesterday collapsed apart
from ownership
new spine seduced by easier
caress
than thinking shadows
thoroughly
full
lingered objects
visibly bewildering loose lips
the folded eyes that yield
at yesterday
that never may exist
that fool
myself declining

1954

ABANDONED BABY

Young ash craven
    never near to gold and
    further still from blood

Birth aborted
    risen in that grave of
    other needs dangling

Angles pins and knobs
    discard their use
    to form your tomb

1957

WHEREAS

Whereas
Judas hung himself
I despise bravura

Whereas
Socrates ignored his wife
I buckle at the brim

Whereas
Judas hung himself
I find no rope as strong

1957

THIS MAN

This old whistle
could not blow
except
to whiskey wheeze
with bandage on his head
temple to temple
black
and dry hands
in his pockets keeping
warm
two trembling fists
clammed
against a stranger
('s) blueandwhite sedan
he
would never drive
could not repair
but damaged
just by standing there.

1964

157: *Towards A Personal Semantics*

FIBROUS RUIN

Fibrous ruin of the skin not near
not anywhere not torn nor stained
now disappears like leaf and flood

A loose appealing
to the vanishing of many scars lost
by long healing of long loss slipped
quietly across a bruise new broken
from new pain inside
the feeling of let go

1965

IF YOU SAW A NEGRO LADY

If you saw a Negro lady
sitting on a Tuesday
near the whirl-sludge doors of
Horn & Hardart on the main drag
of downtown Brooklyn

solitary and conspicuous as plain
and neat as walls impossible to
fresco and you watched her self-
conscious features shape about
a Horn & Hardart teaspoon
with a pucker from a cartoon

she would not understand
with spine as straight and solid
as her years of bending over floors
allowed

skin cleared of interest by a ruthless
soap   nails square and yellowclean
from metal files

sitting in a forty-year-old-flush
of solitude and prickling
from the new white cotton blouse
concealing nothing she had ever noticed
even when she bathed and never
hummed a bathtub tune nor knew one

If you saw her square
above the dirty
mopped-on antiseptic floors
before the rag-wiped table tops

little finger   broad and stiff
in heavy emulation of a cockney

mannerism
would you turn her treat
into surprise
observing

happy birthday

1965

IN MY OWN QUIETLY EXPLOSIVE HERE

In my own quietly explosive here
all silence isolates
to kill the artificial suffocates
a hunger

Likely dying underground
in circles hold together
wings
develop still regardless

1966

159: Towards A Personal Semantics

NOBODY RIDING THE ROADS TODAY

Nobody riding the roads today
But I hear the living rush
far away from my heart

Nobody meeting on the streets
But I rage from the crowded
overtones of emptiness

Nobody sleeping in my bed
But I breathe like windows
broken by emergencies

Nobody laughing anymore
But I see the world split
and twisted up like open stone

Nobody riding the roads today
But I hear the living rush
far away from my heart

FIRING BURST HIS HEAD

Firing burst his head
excruciation blasted silly
clay declining
blind development
exploding fragile like the
afternoon

waste   the steeple placement
flesh too hot to last
or thin
no winner knows
the vulnerable victory arriving

160: Things That I Do in the Dark

dead between the baby hands
unlikely kindred
disappearing

cries around the brighter ravage
relegates an ear alone
an ear afflicted solitary
teach the hollow
formulate crude necrophilia
perhaps

or worse

the phony whining bones
disintegrate to tender tiny now
impossible and true

and true
impossible

1968

OR

OR
like Atlanta parking lots insatiable
and still
collected kindly by the night

love lies

wrong riding hard
in crazy gear
the hills fly by corruptible
and polar up

and up
the bottom traveling
too proud

1968

161: Towards A Personal Semantics

LEAVES BLOW BACKWARD

leaves blow backward with the wind
behind them beautiful
and almost run through atmosphere
of flying birds
or butterflies turn light
more freely than my mouth
learns to kiss by speaking
among aliens.

1968

MAYBE THE BIRDS

Maybe the birds are worried
by the wind

they scream like people
in the hallway

wandering among the walls

1969

POEM TO THE
MASS COMMUNICATIONS MEDIA

I long to fly vast feathers past your mouths on mine
I will to leave the language of the bladder

live yellow and all waste

I will to be

I have begun

I am speaking for

my self

1969

162: Things That I Do in the Dark

OF FAITH: CONFESSIONAL

silence polishing the streets to rain
who walk the waters
side by side

or used to dance apart
a squaretoe solo stunt
apart
ran stubbornly to pantomime
a corpse

show shadows of the deafman
yesterday the breathing broke
to blow some light against the walls

tomorrow drums the body into birth
a symbol of the sun
entirely alive

a birth to darkness

furnace rioting inside the fruit-rim ribs
dogeaten at the garden gate
but better than the other
early bones
that made the dog eat dog
that made the man smash man

catastrophe

far better
better bones

establishing

a second starting
history

a happiness

1969

A POEM FOR ALL THE CHILDREN

The kind of place for sale big cities
where no gateways wide to greet
or terminate the staying there
persist

you keep it
we can corner what we need

The kind of place for sale the price tag
trees the price tag waters of the land the price
tag lighting of a life the cold cash
freeze on filth

                                        o freedom days

The mind or face for sale insensate
supermarket ghostly frozen canned
wrapped-up well-labeled on the counter
always counter-top

The mind or face for sale delivers
hardhead hothouse whoring
homicidal mainly boring
laughter skull

take them things away
we got that   we got that

That place that mind that face
that hereditary rich disgrace

disturbs the triumph
turns the trust disgusting

books that lie and lullabye
school of enemies and fools

the grownup grab thrownup
blownup

long live the child
love bless the wild

lord lord the older deadly life
the deadly older
lord lord

stale dues. no news. no sale

1969

NOT A SUICIDE POEM

no one should feel peculiar living
as they do

next door the neighbors rent their windows

formerly a singing
shatters toneless shards
to line an inmost holdup

drivel salt the stinking coin
iconoclasmic mire
reedy
dull like alcoholic
holy apostolic hireling
herd
inchoate incompatible
and taxing
toll the holy
tell the hireling

          alcoholic
          apostolic
                tales

terrific reeking epidermal
damage
marrow rot

165: Towards A Personal Semantics

sebaceous glisten smell
quotidian kaleidoscopic
tricked indecent darling hell

no one should feel peculiar living well

1970

ROMAN POEM NUMBER ONE

I

Only my own room is gray

from morning on
those high those closing windows
may divide

to make an open wall

(that's maybe nine or ten feet tall)

and when you pulley up the wooden blinds
the outdoor cypress trees
confront
consume
caress the (relatively) small and starving eyes
that mark your face

for love

II

How old is Jesus?

for example well

the dark bronze fountain boy

(behold him)

wet
perpetual

the running water slides his belly loose
the snake around his arm
supplies the slick delectable

the difference

the dry parts where his hard
fat fingers never reach

the area where early light
or late

the boy is there alone

and listening to a sound that is

not his

1970

ROMAN POEM NUMBER FIVE
For Millen and for Julius
and for Peter and for Eddie

I

This is a trip that strangers make
a journey ending on the beach where things
come together like four fingers on his
rather predictable
spine exposed by stars and
when he said this
has never happened before he
meant something
specific to himself because he could not
meet me anywhere inside but
you know

we were both out of the water
both out of it
and really what we wanted was
to screw ourselves into
the place

Pompeii
the Sarno River to the south
the mountain of Vesuvius to the north
the river did not burn
none of the records indicate
a burning river

       of all that went before the earth
       remembers nothing

                     everywhere you see
       the fertility of its contempt
       the sweet alyssum blooming
       in the tomb

       an inward town
well suited to the lives
unraveled and undone
despite the secretly coloring
interior of their suddenly blasted
walls

Vesuvius created and destroyed
             WHOLE TOP OF THE
               MOUNTAIN
             BLOWN OFF
             you can hum some words
             catchy like the title of a song
             (a little song)
             WHOLE TOP OF THE
               MOUNTAIN
             BLOWN OFF
                   (play it again
                   sam)

Pompeii
the mountain truly coming to the men
who used to walk these streets these
sewer drains (the difference is
not very clear)

> juniper and cypress trees
> inspire the dark the only definite the trying
> forms on the horizon sky and sea and the Bay
> of Naples
> single trees
> against abstraction
> trees

the mainstreet moves directly
to the mouth the mountaintop
a vicious puckering

> This is a place where all the lives
> are planted in the ground
> the green things grow
> the other ones
> volcanic victims of an overflow
> a fireflushing tremble
> soul unseasonal
> in rush and rapture
> well they do not grow
> they seed the rest of us
> who prowl
> with plundersucking polysyllables
> to rape the corpse
> to fuck the fallen down and died
> long time ago
> again.

his hand removes some of the sand on my neck
with difficulty

> did the river did the river burn

Pliny the Younger who delivered the volcano
who arrested the eruption into words

excited arrogant terrific
an exclusive
elegant account of mass destruction
79 A.D. that Johnny-on-the-spot say nothing
much about the river and
but eighteen is not too old to worry
for the rivers of the world

                          around the apple flesh and fit
loves holds easily
the hard skin soft enough

                      picture him sweet but cold
                      above the eyebrows
                      just a teenage witness with his pencil
                      writing down disaster

some say
put that apple into uniform
the tree itself wears buttons
in the spring

              VISITING DISASTER IS A WEIRD IDEA
              WHETHER YOU THINK ABOUT IT OR
              NOT

for example limestone the facade the statues the limestone
statues of the everyone of them dead and dead and dead and
no more face among the buried under twenty-seven feet of
limestone other various in general all kinds of dust covering the
dead the finally comfortable statues of the dusty smell today
the nectar fragrance the sun knocks down my meter taking
notes the wheel ruts gutter drains the overhanging upperstories
the timber superstructure the dead the very dead the very very
dead dead farmland pasture dead potato chip dead rooms of
the dead the no longer turbulent blazing the no longer glorious
inglorious the finish of the limestone building limestone statues
look at the wild morninglories red and yellow laughter at the
dying who dig into the death of limestone hard to believe
the guide leads people to the public baths I Bagni di Publicci
to talk about slaves and masters and how many sat at table he
explains the plumbing where men bathed and where the

women (bathed) hot water cold where the wall has a hole in
it or where there is no hole in the wall and the tourists listening
and nobody asks him a question how about the living and the
dead how about that

Pompeii
and we are people who notice the mosaic decorations
of a coffin

we claim to be ordinary men and women or
extraordinary
elbows touching
cameras ready
sensible shoes
architects archaeologists classical
scholars one poet
Black and White and Jewish and Gentile and partly young
and married and once or twice married but
why do we follow
all
inquisitive
confessional or
necrophilomaniac or anyhow
alone
I am not here for you and I will stay there
we are disturbing the peace of the graveyard and
that is the believable limit of our impact
our intent
no
tonight he will hold me hard on the rocks of the ground
if the weather is warm and if
it doesn't rain

2

KEEP MOVING KEEP MOVING

the past is practically
behind us

half skull and teeth
knocked down running an

extreme tilt jerk tilted skull
stiff on its pole plaster cartilage
the legs apart like elbows
then the arms themselves the mouth
of the dead man tense defending still
the visitors peruse these plaster
memories of people
forms created in the cinders
living visitors admire the poise
of agony the poise of agony is
absolute
and who would call it sculpture
raise your own hand to the fire

                    IN THE VILLA DEI
                    MISTERI
                    THERE ARE BLACK
                    WALLS

another plaster person
crouched into his suffocation

yes well in the 14th century B.C.
they·had this remarkable
bedroom where
they would keep one bed
or (some authorities say)
two beds
maybe it was the 15th

                    Pompeii
                    the unfamiliar plain
                    the unfamiliar guilt
                    annihilated men and women who
                    most likely
                    never heard of archaeology of
                    dusty lust

all the possible homes were never built
(repeat)

172: Things That I Do in the Dark

"What's that?"

"That's a whorehouse, honey."

freckle hands chafing together
urbane
he tells the group that in
the declinium
women stayed apart with their loom
(in the declinium

occasional among the rocks the buttercups
obscure until the devil of the land)

       Perhaps Aristotle said the size
       of a city
       should take a man's shout to ears
       even on the edge
       but size never took anything
       much no matter what the porno
       makes believe but
       what will take in the
       scream of a what will
       take it in?

current calculations postulate the
human beings half the size of the market
place

     BEES
     LIZARDS

walls plus walls inhibit action on the lateral
or
with all them walls now how
you gone get next to me

         the falling of ashes
         the rolling lava

the way the things be happening
that garden story figleaf it belong
on top your head

173: Towards A Personal Semantics

they had these industries these
wool and fish sauce
ways to spend the
fooler

even the moon is dark among us
except for the lights by the mountainside
except for the lights

20,000 people
subject
to Vesuvius in natural violence blew
up the handicrafted
fortress spirit of Pompeii
the liquid mangling
motley blood and lava
subject
20,000 people

KEEP MOVING KEEP MOVING

to them the theatre was "indispensable"
seats for 5,000 fabulous acoustics
what
was the performance of the people
in surprise
the rhythm chorus speaking
rescue
multitudes to acrobat survival
one last action on that last
entire stage

today the cypress tree tips dally
wild above the bleachers

when it happened what is happening to us

to hell with this
look at the vegetables blue
in the moonlight

a pinetree colonnade
the wall just under
and the one man made

come to Pompeii
touch my tongue with yours
study the cold formulation of a fearful fix
grid patterns to the streets
the boundaries "unalterable"

the rights of property in stone
the trapezoidal plot the signals
of possession

>   laughter
>   (let's hear it loud)
>   the laughing of the lava
>   tell me
>   stern
>   rigid
>   corpulent
>   stories

the mountains surround the wastebasket bricks of our inquiry

in part
the waters barely stir with poison or with fish

>   I think I know
>   the people who
>   were here
>   where I am

3

my love completely and
one evening anywhere
I will arrive
the right way
given
up to you
and keep no peace

my body sings the force
of your disturbing legs

175: Towards A Personal Semantics

WHAT DID YOU SAY?
NO THANKS.
WHAT DID YOU SAY?

Vesuvius
when Daddy Adam did what he did
the blame the bliss beginning
of no thanks
this is a bad connection
are you serious?

                    the river did not burn

the group goes on
among the bones we travel
light into a new
starvation

                    Pompeii was yesterday
here is Herculaneum
a second interesting testimony
to excuse me but how
will you try to give testimony
to a mountain?

                    there it is baby there it is
                    FURTHER EXCAVATION INTO
                    HERCULANEUM
                    ARRESTED TODAY BY RESSINI living
                    inhabitants impoverished the non-
                    descript Ressini town on top the
                    ruins of

amazing Herculaneum
constructed on an earlier rehearsal flow
of lava maybe
courage or like that a seashore
a resort the remnant spread the
houses under houses
tall trees underlying grass the
pine and palm trees spring toward
Ressini grass retaining walls against the water

176: Things That I Do in the Dark

where there is no water and the sound of children
crying from which city is it Ressini is it
Herculaneum that
does not matter does it is it
the living or the visited the living or
the honored ERCOLANO

                    SUCK
                    SUCK HARD

"Here's where they sold spaghetti"
the leafy sound the feel
of the floor the tile
the painting of a wineglass
a wineglass on the wall unprecedented
turquoise colors would
the red walls make you warm
in winter

            INFORMATION
            WAS
            NOT AVAILABLE
            THE POOR
            OF RESSINI
            REFUSE
            TO COOPERATE
            WITH AUTHORITIES

you better watch out
next summer
and Ressini gone slide
                    down inside them fancy
                    stones
                    and stay there
                    using
                    flashlight
                    or whatever

NOBODY BUDGE
KEEP MOVING KEEP MOVING

                    cabbages cauliflower broccoli
                    the luminous leaves on the land

177: Towards A Personal Semantics

4

yesterday and yesterday
Paestum dates from four
hundred fifty years before the Christ
a fertile lowland calmly naked
and the sky excites the rubble flowers
in between
the mountains and the water
bleaching gentle
in the Middle Ages
mountainstreams came down
and made the meadow into marsh
marble travertine deposits when
the mountains left the land
the memory
deranged the water
turned the plants
to stone

this is the truth the people left this place alone

        we are somewhere wounded by the wind
        a mystery
        a stand deserted by the trees

drizzling rain
destroys the dandelion
and your lips enlarge the glittering
of silence

      Paestum dedicated temples dedicated
      to the terra cotta figurines of trust
      the women in becoming mother of the world
      the midwives hold her arms
      like wings

the river does not burn

      delivering the life

the temple does not stand

still
>PERMISSION GRANTED TO PRESENT
STONE SEX THE ECSTASY OF
PAESTUM

4 main rows of
six in front
the tapering the girth the groove
the massive lifted fit of things
the penis worshiping
fecundity
fecundity
the crepis
stylobate
the cella
columns in entasis
magic
diminution
Doric
flutes
entablature
the leaning
curvilinear
the curve
the profile
magic
elasticity
diameter
effacement

THE TEMPLE IS THE COLOR OF A LIFE

>ON STONE THE SUN CONTINUES
BLISTERING THE SURFACE
TENDERLY

>WHAT TIME IS IT?

as we approach each other
someone else is making
a movie

179: Towards A Personal Semantics

there are horses
one or two beautiful men
and
birds flying
away

1970

ROMAN POEM NUMBER TWELVE

Tim and Johnny run by hoping
to play
off dope "a whole
week
clearing our heads you know
reading science fiction" now
eating an orange not
political
with a magic marker fist
Tim drew on it and
afterward
we move out on the afternoon
a sharing overflow we
play
soccer with a partly broken
pine cone "Hey
man
is that a regulation pine cone?"
"Yeah. God has done it again."

1971

FOR C. G., BECAUSE DAVID CAME
IN HOT AND CRYING FROM THE NEWS

He was still here the friend
the legend
of a good song given
huge
after the commonplace reporting of his death

The film of his smooth
high
outward motion
blurred
the eyelids of the people
who
kept loving him
a
movie in the selfish heart
that will not close
the cameras
        do not record
        a final take
        on living.

ROMAN POEM NUMBER THREE

"I am so sorry to say this but
our poor are not as poor
as yours.
In Italy you will never see the
terrible
sad face the hopelessness
and very dry eyes of America."

181: Towards A Personal Semantics

And now
my teacher turns to bargain
for three small handkerchiefs
to send to Wisconsin for Christmas.

1970

ROMAN POEM NUMBER FOUR

The tiny electrical coffee pot
takes a long time to make
toy bubbles of hot water while
we wait we laugh a lot in a stiff
and a stuffy chair jokes about the world
the war the regular material for
belly laughing through
and "By the way
do you know anyone in Greece? I have/
I had some friends who went there after
the coup. But they have not
written suddenly
for several months and the telephone
operator says that no
such persons as
The Cacoullos
exist."

      —"If you give me the stamps
I will write to somebody who can find out
if your friends are still alive or what."
I hand over the stamps.
It is a good thing sometimes
to buy a few extra.

1971

ROMAN POEM NUMBER SIX

You walk downstairs
to see this man who moves so
quietly in a dark room
where there are balancing
scales on every table.
Signore D'Ettore can tell
you anything about
communications if you mean
the weight the price
of letters
packages
and special post cards.
Hunch-back
short
his grey hair always groomed
meticulous
with a comb and just a touch
of grease
       for three months
he has worn the same well
tailored suit
a grey suit quite unlike
his hair.
       I find it restful
just to watch him making
judgements all of us accept.
"But are you sad?", he asks
me looking up.

"The world is beautiful
but men are bad," he says in
slow Italian.
I smile with him but still the problem
is not solved.
The photographs of Rome
must reach my father but the big
official looking book seems blank

183: Towards A Personal Semantics

the finger-nail of Signore D'Ettore
seems blind and wandering
from line to line among the countries
of a long
small-printed list.
"Jamaica? Where is Jamaica?"
I am silent. My Italian
is not good enough to say, "Jamaica
is an island where you can find
calypso roses sunlight and an old man
my father
on his knees."

1971

ROMAN POEM NUMBER SEVEN

After dinner we take to the streets
let the alleys lead us as they will
into darkness and doorways
regardless
we scratch through the city hot
with wine
our feet our legs as steady
as a kiss on the wall.
In the dress shop
dirty dresses hang idle while
the owner rearranges her own
wool embroidered
heavy legs and plays with the jewelry
someone must have died
to give away.
Her companions make themselves
comfortable with sweat
in the little store
              hustlers

curling sideburns royal
blue wide
wale corduroys packed
smooth in the high
black patent leather boots.
"These jewelry, they are very old.
From Paris. You will like them."
And she hands around the shoebox
graciously.

Two of the men begin to wrestle
each other.
          "Wait!" calls the third.
There is a piece of lint
on the back-slash pocket
of his friend.

1971

ROMAN POEM NUMBER SIXTEEN: SIGHTSEER

Next to me a boy is wearing
a red brocaded velvet jacket

and ragged trousers

in the window
a raw lamb's head
hangs
eyes still in the skull

down the street

we find the Cathedral of Naples
under
extreme repair

185: Towards A Personal Semantics

twisted marble with mosaic
jewels glinting in a cold belt
for a corpse

dwarf women
blowing kisses to the golden altarpiece
or standing
in cheap green cardigans
lace headkerchief
and kissing the wood of the seats
where the faithful
tithe
at the feet of statues
stupid with age

the church delivers the people
from the streets
outside
narrow

a man embraces a sterling silver
pitcher as he emerges from
a grocery store
a girl carries eggs and flowers
children
struggle under boxloads
of
decaying vegetables

humpbacked men and women
limping
overweight
toothless
purulent eyelids
pastry colored cheeks

we
were leaving the church when he said
smiling
"I have a great respect
for the dead. Don't you?"

I didn't answer him.
He must have been speaking
about
his own self-
respect

and
God help him
God
help all of us.

1971

ROMAN POEM NUMBER SEVENTEEN

In their tomb paintings the Greeks reveal
what was important to them
pitchers of wine
supine repose
flute music
leisure
sex
and love

the homosexuals with lyre
one reaching his arm around the other's
head and into his hair his hand
the other boy reaching to caress the
breast of his man
the languid grace
thick lips
sloe eyes

the really comic book depiction
of a man stiffly
diving from a cliff
into water

187: Towards A Personal Semantics

Hippocrates wrote of birth as a breaking
down of the roadway
so that things could move more easily

we may have to die
again
before we can understand
the grace of the dead
but
it may not be worth
the destruction
of a second birth.

1971

ABOUT ENRIQUE'S DRAWING

She lies down a mess
on white paper under glass
a long and a short leg a twisted
arm one good and even
muscular
an okay head
but body in a bloat
impossible

"NO! Not impossible," he says
standing.
"It is
a body.
It is
a structure
that   is not
regular.
Do you see?
No?

Listen:
        ONE
        ONE
        ONE TWO
        THREE FOUR
        ONE
        ONE
        ONETWOTHREE
        ONETWOTHREE
        ONE TWO
        ONETWOTHREE
        ONE TWO
        THREE FOUR
        ONE
        ONE. . . ."

Enrique's body
has become the structure
of a dance. He is real.
And she
the woman lying down a mess
she
has become
mysterious.

1971

ON DIVINE ADAPTATION
TO AN AGE OF DISBELIEF

Watch out.
God is on the tv and the color
and the sex the role
the performance
the everlasting omnipresent
advertised

189: Towards A Personal Semantics

trial
product
cannot de-code
cannot deny
          (Him)
WATCH OUT.

God is on the tv
watching you
and watching me

we

better be

good

1972

ON DECLINING VALUES

In the shadows of the waiting room
are other shadows
beaten
elderly women or
oldfolk bums
depending on your point of view

but
all depending

formerly mothers formerly wives
formerly citizens of some acceptable
position
but
depending and
depending

now exposed unable and unwashed
a slow and feeble crawling through the city
varicose
veins bulging
while the arteries the intake systems
harden
wither
shrivel
close
depending and depending

II

She will leave Grand Central Station
and
depending
spend two hours in St. Patrick's
if the guards there
if police ignore the grovelling length
of time it takes
a hungry woman
just to pray

but here
she whispers
with an aging boyfriend
fugitive and darkblue suited out
for begging who
has promised her a piece
of candy or an orange or an apple
if
they meet tomorrow
if the cops don't chase them separated
wandering under thin
gray hair

III

meanwhile
cops come quick

191: Towards A Personal Semantics

knockbopping up the oakwood benches
BANG
BOP
"GET OUTAHERE," they shout around
the ladies women sisters dying old and all
the formerly wives and mothers
shuffle soft
away
with paper shopping bags beside them

almost empty
and a medium young man
comes up
to ask a question:
"Tell me, I mean, seriously,
how does it feel to be beautiful?"

And I look back at him
a little bit alarmed
a little bit amused
before I say:

"It all depends too much
on you."

1972

ON A MONDAY AFTERNOON

That's me.
I am there.
At the bottom of a closet
among old and used shoes
immobilized
folded at least
in half

in darkness
under old and used clothes
belonging to somebody else.

1974

ON A THURSDAY EVENING

Colossal
The head of the dead
John Kennedy
overlooks all of the citizens
in between acts
drinking champagne
or soda
or anything with bubbles
that will die
fast.

1974

EXCERPTS FROM A VERSE DIARY OF SOMEBODY TRYING TO GET INTO GEAR

for weeks I have been wanting to write this poem
that would muffle my life with the horoscope
of flowers
that would join with rivers rushing along
that would bolt and break up
sentences mid-
bolt and break
impressively

193: Towards A Personal Semantics

like mid-air somersaults
from high-wire freedom
eyes can scarcely capture

to enrapture
whirling words and
abstract dervishes
asplash
  in gutland reappraisal
  of the light we barely share

because for weeks I have been wanting
to make my move
(as the saying goes)
but the travel agents advise
against traveling unarmed
and the route is dark with ideas
I can no longer
calmly
interpret

and this afternoon I noticed
there are more onions than garlic
underneath the sink

will a poem help

me

(*out?*)

1975

FOR THE POET: ADRIENNE RICH

The pheasant arrives
Flemish coloring that burns:
Your word for an eye

1976

194: Things That I Do in the Dark

SOME PEOPLE

Some people despise me be-
cause I have a Venus mound
and not a penis

Does that *sound*
right
to you?

1976

ECOLOGY

When I came back after a few days away
my return terrified a huge
marsh hawk
his new nest next to my front door
Twice that happened:
He explodes with a powerful shuffling
of feathers
aimed in a 45-degree angle that leads
to the sky above the sea
If I go away again
(big as he is)
I wonder which one of us will be

the more surprised?

1976

195: Towards A Personal Semantics

FRAGMENTS FROM A PARABLE
(of the 1950's)

*Paul was Saul. Saul got on the road and the road
and somebody else changed him into somebody else
on the road.*

The worst is not knowing if I do take somebody's
word on it means I don't know and you have to believe
if you just don't know. How do I dare to stand as
still as I am still standing? Arrows create me.
And I despise directions. I am no wish.
After all the lunging still
myself is no sanctuary
birds feed and fly inside me shattering
the sullen spell of my desiring and the
accidental conquest.
Eyeless wings will
twist and sting
the tree of my remaining
like the wind.
   Always there is not knowing, not knowing everything
of myself and having to take whoever you are at your
word. About me.
I am she.

And this is my story of Her. The story is properly yours to
tell. You have created Her, but carelessly. As large as a person,
she nevertheless learns why she walks and the aim of her gaze
and the force of her breath from you who coax her to solve
independently the mystery of your making: Her self.

Your patterns deny parenthood; deny every connection sug-
gesting a connection; a consequence. She cannot discover how
she began nor how she may begin. She seeks the authority of
birth. Her fails. Launched or spinning politely she fails to be-
come her as self unless you allow her a specialty she will accept
as her reason for being. Perhaps you allow her a skill like mercy
or torment. The particular means nothing. Your approval mat-
ters like life and death. She is who I am.
   I am.

My name is me. I am what you call black.

(Only I am still. Arrest me. Arrest me any one or thing. If you arrest me I am yours. I am yours ready for murder or am I yours ready to expose any closed vein. Which is not important. Am I matter to you? Does it? You will try when. But now I am never under arrest. Meanwhile that slit allows me concentration on the bricks black between the windows. I am one of those suffering frozen to the perpetual corrosion of me. Where is the stillness that means?

Here am I holding a pen with two fingers of frenzy of stream of retreat of connection and neurons. Supposedly there is a synapse between things like this: A difference:

between
beyond
beneath
illusions

At least space without pulse. Without illusion: Only I am still: Only I am remaining. I repeat: I am not still: I repeat: Arrest me! You would say mine is a monotone if I could keep my tongue in my fist and my fist in my mouth and my mouth in a glass and that glass in my eyes. But monotony resonates: That would prove how merely am i a complicated position. Or riveted respectably with foot to the ground ignoring the drum and the furnace, the seeds and the water then could I say I am still pretending to be still.

But that complicated position is not. I was simply conceived by something like love. I was simply conceived during the war. My mother was the most beautiful woman in the world. My father was a macro-sperm of lust for that woman painfully asleep on the battlefield. This lust, this loving uncertainty seized three hundred soldiers who paused at her silence as she lay. They made their rabid inquiry and left her.

For almost a year she wandered. For almost a year she wandered with a great song of hatred troubling her lips. She became deranged, an idiot, and everyone adored my mother. Certainly, her song amused them.

At last she struggled to be rid of me. Among the minerals she lay. Silently among the stones of sand she lay. There where the waters begin, like the most elemental mammal she lay. She lay down alone: a small whale. And at the impossible poise between absolute flux and accidental suspense, the most beautiful woman in the world became my mother. But as nothing is absolute nor accidental: I only exchanged equilibria: I was not particularly born.

For days I suckled on the blood of my delivery. Later she learned to ease her breasts and civilized my mouth with milk. No. I played with porpoises. No. Already there is progress. So. Not even then. Not even when beginning. Then is it the beginning not the stillness that means.

If I could eclipse the commencement of the moon. Skip the schedule. Be lunatic and always plunging. Then would I evade the agony of origin. Nor would I suffer an initiation. I would be just an actress, automatic to an action. And that must be how easy. The streets seem mine if I merge with a motion I do not determine. (The fireman slides down a pole. Yes and a siren controls him. There are no obstacle. He attaches himself to the vehicle carrying him. He follows the rules and there are rules how to approach a fire.)

But this is the matter of one step. If I pretend a paralysis am i not seeing? Am I not seeing white cranes idle tonight on the disappearing sidewalk, an empty truck tapered to a spoon that makes the sidewalk disappear, hatchet grass that punctures the pavement, careless carpentry to conceal an incomplete facade, a stairway almost destroyed? But I have reached this random excrement and already my eyes begin a building here at this place of pretended paralysis.

I AM NOT STILL AS i stand here like a phony catatonic:
    aggressively resisting. I am not, it is not important
    am i an impermeable membrane. This resistance
    provokes the madness of enumeration:
        I am insensible to a,b,c,d,e,f,g,—
    And the gamble of elimination:

$$A^x, B^x, C^x\text{---}.$$

The energy this resistance requires is itself an
alteration of temperature, at least.
So I surrender. I surrender and I multiply: Polyblot:

Sponge.
Now am I leaning on a lamppost with metal leaves
and a foundation of dung. Details obliterate within
this light. But I become corpuscular. I AM SEEKING
THE CAPITAL INTRODUCTION TO THE VERY
    FIRST WORD OF
MY MIND. I WANT TO DESTROY IT. I KNOW
    THAT THE VERY
LAST WORD IS NOT ME.
        But I am this moment and corpuscular. I am
that horizontal line laughing at the bottom of the wall.
        I might be the palace protected by the wall.
But I refuse protection: I am better laughing at
the bottom of the wall.
Within this kingdom of the wall is there a king and a palace
gullible to light; gullibility to light despite the infinite opacities
of active men opaque and infinite within this kingdom of the
wall.
The forced stones spread. The town begins to grow among
the bones.

My father came to sanctify my birth; to sanctify the birth of
Her. He came to name my mother, His. He came to tame my
mother and to shelter her. I am supposing.
We will stabilize the sand, he said. We will contain the waters.
We will close the sky. We will squeeze the wind, he said.
                        Build me a wall!
he said that
    He said: We will call this construction by a holy name. The
syllable almost subdued him but he mastered his invention:
masterfully then he said: The House.
    My mother was His. The proud scheme of protection com-
pletely included her. And it was only after he had protected
my mother from experience that he became afraid of the ex-
perience of living with her labyrinthine illusions. Soon he sel-
dom stayed in what he called The House.
    At first such room as he created strangulated us. Then my
mother began to vanish: security is not a color. Paralysis is not
an exercise.

I was learning my father. My father was innocent perhaps: He wanted me to participate in his perseveration of himself: he wanted me to pursue the circle of his escape. And so I left The House and went to walk with him to what he called *the corner of The Wall.*

In that crude culmination, there where the exploitation of silence looks a cobweb, he taught me the way of The Wall.

Worship this thing, he said. Esteem this enemy of impulse. Let the wall become a sacred system for you, the fundamental lie you will believe.

Outside, inside, against, beside The Wall you will hover or hide, or climb, or penetrate, or withdraw. Whatever you choose, your deed will blunder as a dumb show on THE WALL. The absurd, insensible, arbitrary, obstacle qualities of The Wall will annihilate your mind. In this place of The Wall you will discover no necessity to act. The immoveable of your awareness is The Wall. You and what you do are optional. That is the secret, he said, that is the secret of your tragic spontaneity. Be glad you are optional, he told me. His voice was deep. His eyes were shut.

But here am I. Not there. Where am I is there where I am. Here am I. Am I there where nothing is here where nothing is NOW? *I am not here for you and I will stay there.* Now there is nothing but now which is why am I here?

Look at the cloud on the circle.

I am full suddenly full of light.

My father said: There shall be shadow.

I am shining shadows on The Wall.

And my father was only a shadow. His shadow of flesh divulged me: I was an apology of bone.

Anyone is of no consequence. How am I my one?

If I am, I am If in the middle of The Way. The Way leads neither north nor south with possibilities.
Possibilities preclude a wall.
The Way lies in between two walls.
These are the ways of first and last reality.

These are the ways of populous, foul, vertiginous,
predatory, vicious, liquidating, lavatory truth.
The Way is not a transformative via, nor a road for flight from
arrival nor the rhythmic gesture of a street. The Way reveals
only the curb.

It is an intestinal trap: a trick coiled labyrinthine and gut-
teral. I am in the middle of the way.

I am in the middle of a dirty line squeezed by bricks of the
wall precluding possibility. But I am not if I am in the middle
clearly. If I am clearly then am I in the way of nothing.
But I am not alive nor dead.

I am not alive nor dead nor gray nor anything absolute but
I am black. That may mean gamma rays or brown or turd is
another word that may mean brown inside this intestinal trap.
Brown may mean negro. Negro may mean nothing. I am in the
middle of delusion. I am in the way of nothing. But I am in the
way.
My father loved the delusion he sired. The fundamental dream
of my mother, her unnatural ignorance refreshed him and he
surrounded her with new unnecessaries; things that do not
matter, have no matter like The Wall. He gave to her. He gave
of himself to her. He gave gold to her. He told her stories of
herself. He told her the myth of the mirror. He made her the
mirror of myth. He said to my mother many nouns. He said
face and sky and ear and emerald and eye, but then he said
grass. He said she was grass.

My mother wondered what she was. And so he opened the
house.
He gave evening to her and winter.
He gave her alternative illusions.
He gave her a glimpse of endless, enjoyable illusion.
My father opened the house with windows.
I asked my father where was grass Or is there more than my
mother as a metaphor. Around me was my mother and The
Wall and the words my father used to call her as a sound.

I asked my father is there no grass in The House
While we live in The House he said there is no grass
When you have done with living in The House then

when you leave the Wall
when you stop your self
people carry you over THE WALL and bury you under the
grass
Sometimes my father said smiling at me sometimes people bury
you under the grass and near an evergreen tree

I was happy to think of the burial place and I asked my
father to tell me a word for my first dream

He held me on his lap as he gave me the word for my dream
Cemetery was what he whispered in my ear.

I would like to live in that cemetery of trees and grass but he
told me I must go with him struggling for survival until I
finally have done with living in The House.

Then will I be taken to the cemetery And this my father
called A Promise

gulls fly along a shoulder
I am baffled by
your neck concealing
flight

It does not do to say it. And I would not but I cannot do. You
will not let me more than words. I wish that this word were
less than I. I will to be more than this word. You will laughing
let me try. For example, flight.

Three million molecules and marrow but still I will not rise
and am I still. But is there that word. Desire has its sound but is
there a stillness that means. There are wings between my teeth.
Or my mouth consumes some cumulae fuming near my eyes
striated from the hours of the day or garbanzo is a chick-pea.
Still I am still.
Touch my tongue with yours.
I would swallow the limbs of your body and refuse
to Write Down and disturb the magic of my
engorgement.
Let me more than words: I would be more than medium or
limestone. I would be more than looking more than knowing
more
than any of these less than looking less than knowing (*words*)

On the dirt and stones between us was my hand that lay be-
tween us like another stone. Desire has no sound.
I looked the length of more than light at you away from me
Things were hanging   Rosebush maid and
mirror hung. Wires screws hooks and rope were there
Rope no longer green is there in that very long room
I have heard the rope of your throat

I have heard the rope in your throat ready to squeeze
me into the syntax of stone
The sound of my life is a name you may not remember
I am losing the touch of the world to a word

You must have said anything to me

Written from 1958 to 1973